The Internet Revolution

iks are to be returned   before
e

ISSUES

i *ssues*

Volume 158

Series Editor

Lisa Firth

Independence

Educational Publishers
Cambridge

First published by Independence
The Studio, High Green
Great Shelford
Cambridge CB22 5EG
England

© Independence 2008

British Library Cataloguing in Publication Data
The Internet Revolution – (Issues Series)
I. Firth, Lisa II. Series
303.4'833

ISBN 978 1 86168 451 6

Printed in Great Britain
MWL Print Group Ltd

Cover
The illustration on the front cover is by
Simon Kneebone.

CONTENTS

Useful information for readers

Dear Reader,

Issues: The Internet Revolution

In the past two decades, a drastic information revolution has taken place. The advent of the world wide web 15 years ago made the world a smaller place, while today the Internet is increasingly user-driven, with content in the form of blogs, networking sites and wikis. However, as well as being a powerful tool for sharing ideas and information, the Internet can also be a dangerous place. This book looks at Internet trends and online dangers.

The purpose of Issues

The Internet Revolution is the one hundred and fifty-eighth volume in the **Issues** series. The aim of this series is to offer up-to-date information about important issues in our world. Whether you are a regular reader or new to the series, we do hope you find this book a useful overview of the many and complex issues involved in the topic. This title replaces an older volume in the **Issues** series, Volume 104: **Our Internet Society,** which is now out of print.

Titles in the **Issues** series are resource books designed to be of especial use to those undertaking project work or requiring an overview of facts, opinions and information on a particular subject, particularly as a prelude to undertaking their own research.

The information in this book is not from a single author, publication or organisation; the value of this unique series lies in the fact that it presents information from a wide variety of sources, including:

⇨ Government reports and statistics
⇨ Newspaper articles and features
⇨ Information from think-tanks and policy institutes
⇨ Magazine features and surveys
⇨ Website material
⇨ Literature from lobby groups and charitable organisations.*

Critical evaluation

Because the information reprinted here is from a number of different sources, readers should bear in mind the origin of the text and whether the source is likely to have a particular bias or agenda when presenting information (just as they would if undertaking their own research). It is hoped that, as you read about the many aspects of the issues explored in this book, you will critically evaluate the information presented. It is important that you decide whether you are being presented with facts or opinions. Does the writer give a biased or an unbiased report? If an opinion is being expressed, do you agree with the writer?

The Internet Revolution offers a useful starting point for those who need convenient access to information about the many issues involved. However, it is only a starting point. Following each article is a URL to the relevant organisation's website, which you may wish to visit for further information.

Kind regards,

Lisa Firth
Editor, **Issues** series

*Please note that Independence Publishers has no political affiliations or opinions on the topics covered in the **Issues** series, and any views quoted in this book are not necessarily those of the publisher or its staff.*

ISSUES TODAY
A RESOURCE FOR KEY STAGE 3

Younger readers can also now benefit from the thorough editorial process which characterises the **Issues** series with the launch of a new range of titles for 11- to 14-year-old students, **Issues Today**. In addition to containing information from a wide range of sources, rewritten with this age group in mind, **Issues Today** titles also feature comprehensive glossaries, an accessible and attractive layout and handy tasks and assignments which can be used in class, for homework or as a revision aid. In addition, these titles are fully photocopiable. For more information, please visit the **Issues Today** section of our website (www.independence. co.uk).

The Internet

Its history, impact and future. Information from the *Guardian*

By Oliver Burkeman

There are few better ways for anyone over the age of about 25 to experience how it must feel to be extremely old than to reflect on the evolution of computers and the Internet. People who have no memory of any prime minister prior to Margaret Thatcher – let alone of a monarch before Elizabeth II, or an English victory in the World Cup – can easily recall life without email, the web or mobile phones. To think back on the first personal computers in widespread use in Britain is to summon to mind a comically distant time, when cumbersome plastic boxes such as the ZX Spectrum roamed the Earth: machines that were simultaneously revolutionary and yet so feeble as to be incapable of storing more than the equivalent of three emails, or one photograph. (That prehistoric era was 1982, or thereabouts.) The years since the turn of the millennium will be remembered as the decade when we began to grasp the truly transformative psychological implications of living with the Internet.

By 2000, the first dotcom boom was in fact almost over: it ended officially on March 10 2000, when the Nasdaq index peaked, and later plummeted. But ordinary users of the Internet, of whom there were about 370 million at the time, still saw it primarily as a way of retrieving information (via the web) or sending messages to other people (via email). Those amateurs who actually tried to create things in cyberspace tended to restrict themselves to building homepages: self-absorbed mini-biographies that almost nobody else would ever have any reason to read. But all this was beginning to change. In the autumn of 1999, eBay had opened its doors in Britain, and a few months earlier, a software designer, writing on his website in a frivolous mood, had coined the word 'blog'.

The next few months saw a flurry of developments that hinted at the web's potential as a place where real life could be conducted. Friends Reunited, which launched in 2000, was the first encounter most British people had with the concept of social networking, which would later give rise to MySpace (2003) and Facebook (2004). By the end of the year, Friends Reunited had 3,000 users; by the end of the year after that it had 2.5 million. In January 2001, meanwhile, the collaborative encyclopaedia Wikipedia went online; it contained 20,000 articles by the end of 2001 and now boasts 2m. For many people, though, the epitome of what would become known as 'Web 2.0' – meaning an emphasis on interactivity and collaboration online – were blogs. There were about 100,000 in 2002 and 4.8m by 2004. Today, there are more than 70m. But more important, arguably, were the quantities of people reading a small number of highly influential blogs: in 2002, leading political bloggers in the US got their first real taste of power, when their persistence in covering a scandal that might otherwise have faded led directly to the resignation of the Senate majority leader, Trent Lott.

We'll remember the noughties for all these earthquakes, and others – for Google's rise to pre-eminence, and for filesharing, which properly began to threaten the continued survival of the record industry. But underlying them all was a very concrete development: the massive increase in the number of people connected to the Internet via broadband, which finally surpassed the number of people connecting via dial-up in the UK in May 2005. (More than 304 million people now have broadband access worldwide, out of a total of 1.24 billion Internet users, though it's worth remembering that this also shows that any kind of access is still a relative privilege: as of 2007, 81% of the world's population has no home connection.) Broadband finally enabled ordinary people to treat the Internet as a ubiquitous, 'always-on' dimension of their lives, instead of a special place they visited occasionally.

More than 304 million people now have broadband access worldwide, out of a total of 1.24 billion Internet users

---

The irony is that what all this is leading to – the ultimate triumph of the Internet – is the end of 'the Internet' as a meaningfully separate entity. When you can make real money by selling virtual property in Second Life, the boundaries between the two worlds start to blur; when you can navigate to meet a friend at a bar using satellite images on Google Maps via your iPhone, then have a third person join in via video-conferencing software on a WiFi-enabled laptop, it's not clear where online life ends and offline life begins. We'll remember the decade from 2000 as the time when it stopped making sense to think of the Internet as an 'information superhighway', or even as a 'parallel universe', because it became just another way, albeit a staggeringly powerful one, of being human.

2 January 2008

15 years of the world wide web

April 30 2008 was the 15th birthday of the world wide web

April 30 2008 is the 15th birthday of the world wide web; specifically, this date marks the 15th anniversary of CERN (the European Organisation for Nuclear Research) announcing that the web was free for use by anyone. The UK scientist Tim Berners-Lee is individually credited with inventing the web in the course of his work at CERN's headquarters, the world's largest particle physics laboratory, based in Geneva, Switzerland.

The web and the Internet

Although the web and the Internet are different technologies altogether – the web at its core a particular system of interlinked documents, the Internet a vast network of interconnected computers over which the web is accessed – these two are inextricably bound together, all but synonymous in the minds of many.

The web is reliant on the Internet, and the Internet's chief attraction for large numbers of users is the content accessible on, and activities facilitated by, the world wide web. So it is that for many users the web has truly become

By Jane Douglas, Editor, MSN Tech & Gadgets

the 'face' of the Internet.

To commemorate the web's 15th year, Tech & Gadgets looks at 15 ways in which the world wide web has irrevocably changed our lives over the last decade and a half – mostly, though not always, for the better.

15 ways the web changed our lives

1. The rise of online news
The growth and proliferation of web-based news outlets have increasingly brought Internet users online for their daily updates; many are now turning to the web as their primary source of news, rather than the traditional print and television outlets.

2. Global reference library
The web as it was originally conceived by Tim Berners-Lee was an electronic means for researchers to share information across wide geographical areas. Today this is only one of the web's many functions but still a significant one, with reference

material, academic and otherwise, made available to users worldwide.

3. Plagiarism
A natural flipside to a world of easily accessible information is the plagiarism that is just a quick copy and paste away. With online encyclopaedias such as Wikipedia at the fingertips of school kids and students around the world, web-enabled cheating is an ever-present temptation. Some universities have accordingly brought in software to scan essays and reports for tell-tale signs of copied web material.

> **Despite concerted efforts by various governments to suppress and censor what appears on the web, this kind of total control has proved to be very difficult indeed**

4. Search engines
Ever more sophisticated search engines shape the way in which the world experiences the web, and very few sessions on the web are complete without a search or two. For those of us who chiefly rely on these devices to discover websites, it is the search engine that decides what we end up looking at.

5. Liberating information and opinion
Despite concerted efforts by various governments to suppress and censor what appears on the web, this kind of total control has proved to be very difficult indeed. The web has made information and opinion, particularly political opinion, all but internationally irrepressible.

6. Blogs

The blog – a cornerstone of the emphatically interactive web 2.0 – gave a voice to formerly silent web users the world over. Suddenly web presences were not just for corporations and shops but effortlessly available to all, and for whatever purpose: from the worthy causes of activism, politics and citizen journalism to simple web-based diaries and oddball Internet humour.

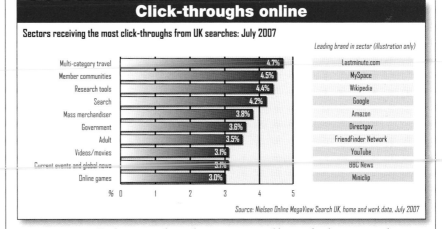

Click-throughs online

Sectors receiving the most click-throughs from UK searches: July 2007

Leading brand in sector (illustration only)

Sector	%	Leading brand
Multi-category travel	4.7%	Lastminute.com
Member communities	4.5%	MySpace
Research tools	4.4%	Wikipedia
Search	4.2%	Google
Mass merchandiser	3.8%	Amazon
Government	3.6%	Directgov
Adult	3.5%	FriendFinder Network
Videos/movies	3.1%	YouTube
Current events and global news	3.1%	BBC News
Online games	3.0%	Miniclip

Source: Nielsen Online MegaView Search UK, home and work data, July 2007

Online video, radio, television, music and games have all drastically altered the way in which we consume entertainment

---

7. Webmail

Though e-mail is not strictly a web technology, the overwhelming popularity of webmail has obviously revolutionised the way we communicate with each other, allowing users to access their inboxes via straightforward websites from any Internet-accessing computer they can get their hands on.

8. Social networking

Another pervasive web 2.0 innovation, social networking sites like Facebook and Bebo have helped countless web users make new friends and catch up with old ones.

9. World wide distraction

Though originally intended for sharing knowledge, the web has proved to be quite as effective as an endless distraction from the things on which we are supposed to be concentrating. Perhaps it is best that we do not know the sum total of hours collectively lost to trawling the web for useless trivia.

10. Shopping through your browser

Online shopping – not to mention online auctions, banking, price comparison sites and customer reviews – has shaken up the retail and commercial sectors in a way that would have been barely imaginable before the birth of the web, empowering web-based consumers everywhere.

11. Online identity theft

Partly a repercussion of the above point, the amount of personal data shared over the web – and the way in which it is made secure and private – is a serious concern. Malware, spyware and plain old poor data security have had us thinking twice about what we are willing to share with a website.

12. Digital entertainment

Online video, radio, television, music and games have all drastically altered the way in which we consume entertainment – entertainment that traditionally belonged to offline media and formats. The way in which we have enthusiastically embraced streaming and downloads has got the music, film and television industries each wanting in on the action – or struggling to keep up.

13. Entertainment of the adult variety

With a more-than-sizeable chunk of the web solely dedicated to adult content of all varieties, no discussion of the web could be complete without a mention of pornography. The world wide web has certainly transformed access to supposedly adults-only material.

14. Time shrinking

The web has had a major hand in increasing our expectation of instant gratification – and our general impatience.

If you wanted to track down information in days gone by, you might have called up directory enquiries, gotten a phone number, rung the number, waited to speak to someone, then spent five minutes on the phone requesting that something be sent to you by post. You would then quite happily wait two or three days for it to turn up. Now this three-day operation can be crammed into about three minutes at most.

15. Online travel booking

Where would budget airlines be without the world wide web? With web users increasingly booking their flights and holidays online, long gone are the days of traipsing to Thomas Cook and struggling home with 32 different glossy brochures.

30 April 2008

⇨ The above information is reprinted with kind permission from MSN Tech and Gadgets. Visit http://tech.uk.msn.com for more information.

© MSN

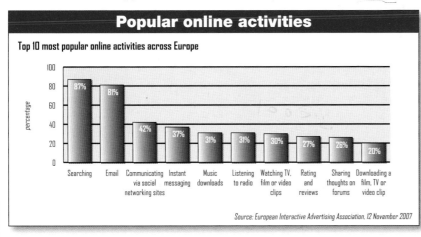

Popular online activities

Top 10 most popular online activities across Europe

Activity	percentage
Searching	87%
Email	81%
Communicating via social networking sites	42%
Instant messaging	37%
Music downloads	31%
Listening to radio	31%
Watching TV, film or video clips	30%
Rating and reviews	27%
Sharing thoughts on forums	26%
Downloading a film, TV or video clip	20%

Source: European Interactive Advertising Association, 12 November 2007

The communications revolution

UK benefits from communications anytime, anywhere and at a lower cost

Ofcom today published its annual Communications Market Report 2007 which reveals new trends in the UK's £50bn electronic communications sector.

UK consumers now spend 50 hours per week on the phone, surfing the Internet, watching television or listening to the radio. Average daily Internet use in 2006 (36 minutes) was up 158% on 2002 and time spent on the mobile phone (almost 4 minutes per day) was up 58%. Time spent watching TV was down 4% at 3 hours and 36 minutes, listening to radio was down 2% at 2 hours and 50 minutes and time spent on a fixed line phone was down 8% at 7 minutes.

While consumers are getting more out of their communications services, the amount they are spending on them continues to fall. In 2006, average household spend on communications services was £92.65 per month, down from £94.03 in 2005.

Ofcom's 330-page report shows how consumers are using new digital communications services to take control of how, when and where they access and use communications services. In particular:

⇨ The range of services and devices now available to children (8- to 15-year-olds) in the UK is rapidly

changing what they do with their time. Over 75% of 11-year-olds now have their own television, games console and mobile phone. Some 15% of 13- to 15-year-olds and 7% of 10-year-olds also have their own webcam.

⇨ Fewer children are playing console and computer games (61% regularly did so in 2005, down to 53% in 2007), watching videos and DVDs (59% did so regularly in 2005 and 38% in 2007) and listening to radio (40% listened regularly in 2005 and 20% in 2007). Instead, they are using their mobile phones more often (50% regularly did so in 2005 compared with 53% in 2007), surfing the Internet (47% regularly in 2005 to 52% in 2007) and using MP3 players (20% regularly in 2005 to 28% in 2007).

⇨ Older people are also consuming more media. The over-55s was

the only age group to increase its average radio listening between 2002 and 2007 (up 5.5%). And older people are not just increasing their use of traditional media. Some 16% of over-65s use the web. These silver surfers spend an average of 42 hours online every month, more than any other age group. Indeed, far from being just a young person's technology, one-quarter of all UK Internet users are over 50 and the over-50s account for 30% of total time spent online.

⇨ Among 25- to 34-year-olds, women spend more time using the Internet than men. In this age group, 2.18m young women users account for 55% of total time spent online. By comparison, just 1.83m 25- to 34-year-old men in the UK use the Internet.

The networked nation

The process of convergence – bringing technologies, platforms and devices closer together – is connecting the nation as never before. Consumers can now get live TV over their mobile, radio over their TV and make voice calls on the Internet.

⇨ There is now an even greater range of 'bundled' communications services providing landline, broadband, digital television and mobile in a single package. As a result, the number of consumers taking services in bundles rose to 40% of the population by April 2007, up by a third over 12 months.

⇨ Consumers are increasingly using telephone services over the Internet offered by so-called VoIP providers. At the end of 2006 20% of respondents to Ofcom's survey said they were phoning online, up from 14% at the end of 2005.

⇨ And in the UK we are increasingly

relying on our mobile phones. The report shows that by the end of 2006 there were more than double the number of mobile connections (69.7m) than landline connections (33.6m). More UK households now rely just on a mobile phone (9%) than rely just on a landline (7%) and for the first time, total mobile call minutes (82bn) accounted for over one-third of all call minutes (234bn).

⇨ Today's consumers are using their mobiles for much more than just making phone calls. Some 41% of mobile phone users regularly use their phone as a digital camera, 13% use it for Internet access, 10% listen to FM radio broadcasts, and 21% use it as a mini games console. And in 2006 mobile users in the UK sent 20% more texts than the previous year, with an average of 12 text messages per mobile per week.

⇨ Wireless networks are allowing more people to access the Internet on-the-move. Some 11.2% (7.8m) of mobile phones now connect to a 3G network (70% up on 2005 at 4.6m). The report also shows the number of Wi-Fi hotspots in the UK, which enable broadband-speed wireless Internet access, is increasing. By April 2007 there were 11,447 hotspots compared to 10,339 a year previously.

⇨ Digital television – in 80.5% per cent of UK homes by April 2007 – is changing what, when and how we watch. One of the new services being used by viewers in the 11.5 million subscription television households is high-definition (HD) television. The report finds that, in the 450,000 homes that have it, 33% of viewing time is spent watching in HD and 43% of those surveyed said that they watch more television – especially premium content such as films and sport – as a result of having HD.

⇨ And by April 2007, 15% of respondents said they had a digital video recorder (DVR), almost double the number at the end of 2006. DVRs allow users to record whole television series and to pause and rewind live programmes.

⇨ Radio listeners have a much wider choice of stations and ways of listening due to the growth of digital radio. In 2006 the total number of DAB digital radio sets sold broke through the 5 million mark and 17.2% of UK homes now have a DAB digital radio. DAB sets accounted for 18.6% of all radio sales in 2006 (1.8m sets) compared to 12.9% in 2005 (1.5m sets).

Over 75% of 11-year-olds now have their own television, games console and mobile phone. Some 15% of 13- to 15-year-olds and 7% of 10-year-olds also have their own webcam

---

⇨ DAB is not the only way that consumers listen to digital radio. The report finds that 33% of consumers have listened to the radio via digital television (15% do so at least weekly), 21-22% listen online (12% at least weekly) and 10-12% listen via their mobile phone (6% at least weekly).

A changing industry

Increased convergence of services and technologies is also changing the shape of the communications sector and in particular industry revenues.

Television

⇨ UK television advertising revenue in 2006 fell by 2.2% on the previous year to £3.5bn, the first fall since 2002. The decline in advertising revenues coincides with greater availability and use of television-style content online and the growth of digital video recorders (DVRs) that allow users to skip adverts, putting even greater pressure on advertising revenues. The report found that up to 78% of DVR owners regularly used them to skip through adverts.

⇨ Declining advertising revenue is, however, increasingly being supplemented by alternative sources of income. In 2006 subscription revenues increased to £4bn (approximately £350 per subscription), up from £3.3bn in 2005. Similarly, revenues from interactive services, such as quiz television channels and participative voting in programmes, increased by 18.3% during 2006 to £123m, although this new source of income may be affected in the future as broadcasters review their approach to interactive TV.

⇨ While television advertising overall is declining, revenues for digital-only free-to-air channels, such as ITV2, More4 and Five Life, is rising and for the first time broke though the £1bn mark in 2006, a 21% increase over 2005. Revenue for the three commercial terrestrial channels – ITV1, Channel 4 and Channel 5 – stood at £2.4bn in 2006, 9.6% lower than in 2005.

⇨ As television advertising revenue declines, online advertising spending continues to surge, up 47% during 2006 and just breaking the £2bn mark. Internet advertising spend is now equivalent to almost half (44%) that spent on all TV advertising, to 83% of advertising spend on ITV1, Channel 4 and Five and to one-quarter (24.2%) of all press advertising.

Telecoms and broadband

⇨ By April 2007 53% of UK households had a broadband connection. Headline broadband speeds – the maximum advertised speed of a service – have doubled over the last 12 months. The average blended headline broadband speed stood at 3.6Mbit/s at the end of 2006 compared to 1.6Mbit/s in the previous year. By June 2007 this had risen to 4.6Mbit/s.

⇨ The increase in headline speeds is due in part to continued investment and growth in local loop unbundling which enables operators to install their own equipment in BT's exchanges and offer broadband services direct to consumers. There has been a threefold increase in the proportion of properties connected to an unbundled telephone exchange which are actually taking an unbundled service, from 3% in March 2006 to 9% in March 2007. Average headline speeds are also being boosted by ongoing investment in infrastructure on both the BT and cable networks.

⇨ Competition in the provision of phone services is also increasing. Whilst BT is diversifying its revenue streams in other areas, its share of fixed voice call volumes fell below 50% for the first time in 2006 (48%) and the company's share of all telecoms connections (including mobile) fell below one in four (23%, down from 26% a year ago).

⇨ Increased competition is driving down prices for consumers. Ofcom's analysis of the cost of a typical basket of residential telecoms services (including a fixed line, two mobiles and a broadband connection per household, all at 2006 usage levels) shows that consumers would have paid £6.51 (9%) more for the same bundle of services in 2005 than in 2006. In the five years to 2006 the cost saving on the same bundle was £34.97 in real terms.

Radio

⇨ While the total number of radio stations in the UK has increased through the expansion of DAB (in June 2007 there were 389 radio stations in the UK, 169 of which were available on DAB), the report shows that the total number of radio listening hours declined to an average of 19.8 hours per week per listener in 2006. This fell further to 19.4 hours in Q1 2007. This decline has been felt most in the commercial local radio sector. Between April 2005 and April 2006, average listening to local commercial radio fell by 4.1%.

⇨ As listening has declined, so has commercial radio advertising revenue. Between 2001 and 2006, radio's share of total advertising revenue in the UK fell by 14.3% and in 2006 stood at £480m. Total revenue for local commercial stations fell by 9.5% from £169m in 2005 to £153m in 2006.

⇨ By contrast, the report finds that people are increasingly tuning in to BBC radio. In the first three months of 2007, four out of the five most listened-to stations were all BBC. The top five were: BBC Radio 2, Radio 1, Radio 4, Classic FM and Five Live.

⇨ The report also estimates that the BBC's expenditure on radio, at £637m in 2006, is at its highest level in five years. This compares to £512m for the commercial radio sector, at its lowest level since 2002.

Ofcom Partner of Strategy and Market Developments, Peter Phillips, said: 'This comprehensive survey shows how our communications sector continues to develop at a fast pace, with consumers of all ages using a range of devices to find the services they want at lower prices.' He added: 'Industry innovation and competition continue to deliver significant benefits to the UK economy and consumers.'

The full report is available online at: www.ofcom.org.uk/research/cm/cmr07
23 August 2007

⇨ The above information is reprinted with kind permission from Ofcom. Visit www.ofcom.org.uk for more information.

© *Ofcom*

Web 2.0

Information from the Sharpened Glossary

Web 2.0 is a term that was introduced in 2004 and refers to the second generation of the world wide web. The term '2.0' comes from the software industry, where new versions of software programs are labelled with an incremental version number. Like software, the new generation of the web includes new features and functionality that was not available in the past. However, Web 2.0 does not refer to a specific version of the web, but rather a series of technological improvements.

Some examples of features considered to be part of Web 2.0 are listed below:

⇨ Blogs – also known as web logs, these allow users to post thoughts and updates about their life on the web.

⇨ Wikis – sites like Wikipedia and others enable users from around the world to add and update online content.

⇨ Social networking – sites like Facebook and MySpace allow users to build and customise their own profiles and communicate with friends.

⇨ Web applications – a broad range of new applications make it possible for users to run programs directly in a web browser.

Web 2.0 technologies provide a level of user interaction that was not available before. Websites have become much more dynamic and interconnected, producing 'online communities' and making it even easier to share information on the web. Because most Web 2.0 features are offered as free services, sites like Wikipedia and Facebook have grown at amazingly fast rates. As the sites continue to grow, more features are added, building off the technologies in place. So, while Web 2.0 may be a static label given to the new era of the web, the actual technology continues to evolve and change.

⇨ The above information is reprinted with kind permission from the Sharpened Glossary. Visit www.sharpened.net/glossary for more information.

© *Sharpened Glossary*

Internet's a family affair

EIAA research shows massive opportunity to engage with digital families

Research announced today from the European Interactive Advertising Association (EIAA) reveals that adults who live with children are more engaged online than those who don't, indicating that family needs and wants are shaping web behaviour.

Almost three-quarters (73%) of people living with children are logging on to the Internet each week, compared with only half (52%) of those without

---

The first ever 'Digital Families' Report, the latest in the EIAA Mediascope Europe series, reveals interesting insights into the digital lifestyles of Europe's online families. The research shows that almost three-quarters (73%) of people living with children are logging on to the Internet each week, compared with only half (52%) of those without. They are also engaging in a wider range of digital activities than those that live without children, ever extending the depth and complexity of their experience. This increases the opportunity for brands to engage with their audience online and means that marketers must develop targeted and effective online strategies to appeal to today's online families and meet their specific lifestyle needs.

Influencing entertainment

Almost a third (30%) of these digital parents are watching film, TV or video clips online, demonstrating how entertainment is becoming integral to the family Internet experience. It's an activity which is growing enormously in popularity (+150% since 2006) and with 22% also intending to upgrade to broadband in the next six months,

this trend is set to accelerate. 32% are listening to the radio online and 66% now regularly use the Internet as a source of news – showing how broadcast and other traditional media are increasingly being consumed online.

In addition, digital parents are using the Internet to express themselves more and to interact with others. Web activities such as ratings and reviews and creating and sharing content have experienced a significant boost since 2006 (+40% and +27% respectively).

Age differences

The research also shows that the websites visited by digital parents and their online activities vary according to the age of the children. People living with very young children (between nought and four) are increasingly visiting health and film websites (+24% since 2006) while those living with children between five and nine are going to games sites (+32%). Price comparison sites are seeing a boost amongst those living with children between ten and fifteen (+31%) while those with

older children (between 16 and 18) are enjoying more TV sites (+77%). Users living with older children also seem to be more technically advanced – almost half (47%) of those living with children aged 16-18 use instant messaging services compared to 37% of people living with children aged nought to four. A similar trend is seen when comparing film, TV or video clip downloads (30% vs. 22%) and music downloads (36% vs. 32%).

Gadgets and games

Overall, the study demonstrates that people living with children are more technologically aware and advanced due to their heightened experience of, and exposure to, gadgets and gizmos.

People living with children are also more likely than those without to use a mobile phone, PDA or blackberry (91% vs. 83%) and to actively engage in a wide range of mobile phone functions – further indicating the influence of youth on technical skill and openness to adopt. More than half (53%) have taken a photo or video clip (vs. 37% of those without children), 12% have surfed Internet

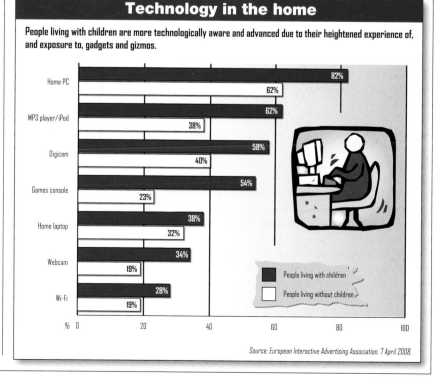

Technology in the home

People living with children are more technologically aware and advanced due to their heightened experience of, and exposure to, gadgets and gizmos.

Technology	People living with children	People living without children
Home PC	82%	62%
MP3 player/iPod	62%	38%
Digicam	58%	40%
Games console	54%	23%
Home laptop	38%	32%
Webcam	34%	19%
Wi-Fi	28%	19%

■ People living with children
□ People living without children

Source: European Interactive Advertising Association, 7 April 2008.

sites (vs. 9%) and 8% have watched video or film clips on their mobiles (vs. 5%).

Family time online

Overall, digital parents are ramping up their web time, spending 11.6 hours online each week (up 36% since 2004) and over a quarter are heavy users of the Internet (27%). Digital families are also more likely than those households without children to use the Internet at the weekends (58% vs. 40%).

This online activity has meant that digital families are consuming other media less as a result of the Internet – 44% of digital parents are watching less TV, almost a third read fewer magazines and newspapers (31% and 30% respectively) and almost a quarter (24%) listen to the radio less.

This can be attributed in part to the fact that time-pressured adults living with children find the web provides what they want quickly and saves them time (76% vs. 68% of people without children) while almost half (47%) believe it puts them in control (vs. 42%).

Alison Fennah, Executive Director of the EIAA, says, 'Looking at the online habits and activities of digital families highlights just how inclusive and engaging the Internet has become. Marketers have traditionally tracked youth as a demographic online so it is particularly interesting to see their influence on the rest of the family. Whether it's time-pressures, information accessibility or entertainment needs that prompt use, online has a very clear part to play in the daily lives of each and every member of the family, whether surfing solo or together as a unit. Marketers must look to tap into this mindset when creating online campaigns.'

Note

The study involved 7,008 random telephone interviews with over 1,000 respondents in the UK, Germany, France, Spain, Italy and the Nordics respectively and 500 respondents in Belgium and the Netherlands respectively. Interviews were conducted throughout September 2007. 7 April 2008

⇨ The above information is re-printed with kind permission from the European Interactive Advertising Association. Visit www.eiaa.net for more information.

© EIAA

Blogging

Find out what it is, how to set up a blog for yourself and how others are using blogs to get their messages heard

What is blogging?

Blogging is a simple way of getting your voice heard online. A blog (or 'weblog') can be used for a whole range of reasons. Professional and amateur journalists use them to discuss news or events, others use blogs to air their views, discuss their hobbies or as a kind of diary to record their thoughts, experiences and everyday life.

How can I do it?

You don't need any special equipment or software to blog. All you need is a connection to the Internet, an opinion and a site to host your blog. There are lots of websites which will host your blog. To get started, find yourself a host and follow their setup advice and start writing. It really is that simple! You can add photos, videos, sound clips, links to your favourite websites or other bloggers' pages.

How can I use a blog to promote my message?

Many people use their blog as a tool to expose misconduct or problems within their organisation, others offer an insight into the workings of government or politics. Young volunteers or activists often use them as a diary of how their project or cause is progressing and as a way to gain publicity and a following for their work. Blogs written by everyday people are also valuable to journalists reporting on restricted or war-torn countries.

With more than 100 million blogs online, the most difficult part is accessing an audience. The best approach is to target a particular audience and publicise your blog and its topics through your own networks. Building up regular readers will help to widen your audience.

Are there any downsides?

Although blogs can be anonymous, they're still subject to the law, so be careful publishing entries that could be damaging to someone, or which contain confidential information. You should also bear this in mind when reading other blogs; do they use any evidence for their ideas or is it just their opinion?

If your blog isn't receiving many comments it can feel like you're blogging for yourself. Building an audience is hard work and can take time, so be patient, keep blogging and get your blog linked on as many other blogs and sites as you can.

Examples of successful blogs

do-it.org.uk's volunteering blogs – Follow the lives of different volunteers, from students and campaigners to people volunteering abroad.

Global Voices Online aggregates global blogs to showcase places and people other media often ignore. Here you'll find a wealth of blogs from all around the world selected, written or translated by the website's own group of editors and volunteers.

The Guerilla Gardening Blog reports on a group of gardeners who transform barren areas of London into blooming gardens – often in the middle of the night! This blog allows you to follow the group's movements, with pictures to help illustrate the cause.

⇨ The above information is re-printed with kind permission from TheSite. Visit www.thesite.org for more information.

© TheSite

Ofcom research identifies social networking profiles

Information from Directgov

Nearly half of all children who have access to the Internet have their own personal profile on a social networking site, according to Ofcom research published today.

Over a fifth (22%) of adult Internet users aged 16+ have their own online profile

---

The report reveals just how quickly social networking sites have become a part of Britons' lives. As well as widespread use amongst 8- to 17-year-olds (49% of Internet users in that age group), the report also reveals that over a fifth (22%) of adult Internet users aged 16+ have their own online profile.

The research finds that it is common for adults to have a profile on more than one site and half of current adult social networkers say that they access their profiles at least every other day.

The research also shows how social networking sites are stretching the traditional meaning of 'friends'. Some users say that they derive enjoyment from 'collecting' lists of people with whom they have an online connection but often have never met.

Types of social networkers

The qualitative research suggests five distinct groups of people who use social networking sites:

⇨ Alpha Socialisers – mostly male, under 25s, who use sites in intense short bursts to flirt, meet new people and be entertained.
⇨ Attention Seekers – mostly female, who crave attention and comments from others, often by posting photos and customising their profiles.
⇨ Followers – males and females of all ages who join sites to keep up with what their peers are doing.
⇨ Faithfuls – older males and females generally aged over 20, who typically use social networking sites to rekindle old friendships, often from school or university.
⇨ Functionals – mostly older males who tend to be single-minded in using sites for a particular purpose.

The research also suggests three distinct groups of people who do not use social networking sites:

⇨ Concerned about safety – often older people and parents concerned about safety online, in particular making personal details available online.
⇨ Technically inexperienced – often people over 30 years old who lack confidence in using the Internet and computers.
⇨ Intellectual rejecters – often older teens and young adults who have no interest in social networking sites and see them as a waste of time.

Privacy and safety

Despite being one of the main reasons cited by some respondents for not using social networking sites, privacy and safety are not a top of mind concern for those who use social networking sites. The research found that:

⇨ 41 per cent of children and 44 per cent of adults leave their privacy settings as default 'open' which means that their profiles are visible to anyone;
⇨ 34 per cent of 16- to 24-year-olds are willing to give out sensitive personal information such as their phone number or email address;
⇨ 17 per cent of adult users said that they talked to people on social networking sites that they didn't know and 35 per cent spoke to people who were 'friends of friends'.

2 April 2008

⇨ The above information is reprinted with kind permission from Directgov. Visit www.direct.gov.uk for more information.

© Crown copyright

The growth of social media sites

UK's most popular social media websites: Jan 2008.

Rank J08	Rank J07	Website	UK unique audience (000s) Jan 08	UK unique audience (000s) Jan 07	Change in UA Jan 07-Jan 08	Social media type
1	2	YouTube	10,426	6,667	56%	Video
2	1	Wikipedia	9,557	7,758	23%	Information
3	18	Facebook	8,513	1,048	712%	Network
4	4	Blogger	5,145	3,697	39%	Blogging
5	3	MySpace	5,026	5,513	-9%	Network
6	8	Bebo	4,090	2,670	53%	Network
7	16	Slide	3,355	1,092	207%	Add-on tool
8	10	Yahoo! Answers	3,319	2,111	57%	Information
9	6	Windows Live Spaces	3,127	2,716	15%	Network
10	9	TripAdvisor	2,364	2,186	8%	Travel reviews

Source: Nielsen Online, UK NetView, home & work data, including applications, Jan 2007-Jan 2008.

Social networking and your electronic footprint

4.5 million young Brits' futures could be compromised by their electronic footprint. Survey reveals extent of online content that could damage the prospects of young people and leave many more vulnerable to identity fraud

Quotes from young people

Some quotes from young people when told that the information they put online could still be there in 5, 10 or 20 years:

⇨ 'I think it is quite daunting as it could hinder my career choice' (female, 19, West Mids)

⇨ 'I had a blog a couple of years ago and want to delete it – but I can't, and I had personal details on it!' (female, 16, Yorks)

⇨ 'Potential employers could "google" you and it could give embarrassing information etc' (male, 16, NW)

⇨ 'It sort of scares me to think that what I've written at my age now (17) may come back to haunt me in later years. I did not know this' (female, 17, NW)

⇨ 'Initial thoughts – who cares? Subsequent thoughts – omg!!!' (female, 14, Scotland)

⇨ 'Really annoying, a search on google brings up stuff I put online when I was really young and I can't get rid of it' (male, 16, SE)

As many as four and a half million* young people (71%) would not want a college, university or potential employer to conduct an Internet search on them unless they could first remove content from social networking sites, according to new research by the Information Commissioner's Office (ICO). But almost six in ten have never considered that what they put online now might be permanent and could be accessed years into the future.

The research findings are unveiled as the ICO launches a new website at www.ico.gov.uk/youngpeople to help young people understand their information rights. The first section contains tips and advice on safe social networking.

As well as not thinking ahead before posting information on the web, the survey of Britons aged 14-21** also revealed that youngsters' online behaviour is a gift to potential fraudsters. Two-thirds (eight in ten girls aged 16-17) accept people they don't know as 'friends' on social networking sites and over half leave parts of their profile public specifically to attract new people. More than seven in 10 are not concerned that their personal profile can be viewed by strangers and 7% don't think privacy settings are important and actively want everyone to see their full profile.

As for the data that young people make available, 60% post their date of birth, a quarter post their job title and almost one in ten give their home address. Couple this basic information with details that might be used to create passwords e.g. sibling's name (posted by 23%), pet's name (posted by a quarter of girls) and even mother's maiden name (posted by 2%) and fraudsters have the information they need to obtain products and services in a young person's name or access existing bank or online accounts.

David Smith, Deputy Commissioner for the ICO, said: 'Many young people are posting content online without thinking about the electronic footprint they leave behind. The cost to a person's future can be very high if something undesirable is found by the increasing number of education institutions and employers using the Internet as a tool to vet potential students or employees.

The research also found that a third of young people have never read privacy policies on social networking sites and don't understand how

Protecting your identity online – ICO top tips

⇨ A blog is for life... remember you risk leaving a permanent electronic footprint. If you don't think you'll want it to exist somewhere in 10 years' time, don't post it.

⇨ Privacy is precious – choose sites that give you plenty of control over who can find your profile and how much information they can see. Read privacy policies and understand how sites will use your details.

⇨ Personal safety first – don't allow people to work out your 'real life' location e.g. your place and hours of work. Your personal safety offline could be affected by what you tell people online.

⇨ Password protected – change your passwords regularly, don't use obvious words like your pet's name and don't use the same passwords on social networking sites as you do for things like Internet banking.

⇨ Address aware – use a separate email address for social networking and one that doesn't give your year of birth or ideally, your full name.

⇨ Reputation is everything – what seems funny to you and your friends now might not be to your teachers, university admissions tutor or prospective employer – or to you in years to come.

they can manage their personal information. But when asked how they feel about websites potentially using their details to target advertising

---

Almost six in 10 young people have never considered that what they put online now might be permanent and could be accessed years into the future

---

at them or to pass on to other websites or brands, a huge 95% are concerned about this, with 54% caring 'a lot' about how their personal information is used.

David Smith continues: 'This shows that when young people are made aware that their details could be being passed between parties – legitimate or unscrupulous – they are worried. We have to help teenagers wise up to every aspect of the Internet age they're living in – it may be fun but unfortunately it is not the safe space many think it is.'

Notes

* Based on UK population aged 14-21 in 2006 of 6,415,800 and 71% of survey respondents indicating that either there is 'some' or 'a lot' of online content on social networking sites, chatrooms or blogs they would not want found by a person in authority. From Office of National Statistics: http://www.statistics.gov.uk/StatBase/Expodata/Spreadsheets/D9657.xls

** Survey of 2,000 14- to 21-year-olds conducted by Dubit in October 2007.

⇨ The above information is re-printed with kind permission from the Information Commissioner's Office and is taken from a press release document. Visit www.ico.gov.uk for more information.

© Crown copyright

Social networking is going mobile

One in four members of UK social networks use their phones to network

Nielsen Mobile, a service of The Nielsen Company, today reveals how UK mobile phone subscribers are taking online social networking beyond the home and office.

⇨ Almost half (44%) of UK mobile phone subscribers belong to an online social network. Of this group, one in four (25%) use their mobile phone for social networking-related activities.

⇨ Around 812,000 Britons each month, or 1.7% of all UK mobile subscribers, visited a social networking website using their mobile during the first quarter of 2008.

⇨ Facebook is the most popular site for mobile social networking, being visited by over half a million Britons (557,000) from their mobiles, or 9% of all UK mobile Internet subscribers.

Kent Ferguson, Client Services Manager, Nielsen Mobile: 'Social networking is already a global phenomenon, and mobile could be the next big thing in the space. Large numbers of people are interacting with their social networking profiles while they're on the move. There could be increased consumer demand for mobile social networking driven by the flat fee price plans offered by the leading operators that give subscribers unlimited mobile Internet access.'

Mobile vs. PC – how the leading social networks compare

⇨ The four most popular social networks on the mobile are also the four most popular on the PC.

⇨ Travel social network WAYN has the strongest performance on the mobile compared to the PC, ranking 7th on mobile Internet compared to 21st on PC Internet.

Social networking and mobile phones

Most popular social networks on UK mobile phones.

Rank	Social network	Unique mobile subscribers (000s)	% mobile internet reach	PC internet rank
1	Facebook	557	9.0%	1
2	MySpace	211	3.4%	2
3	Bebo	162	2.6%	3
4	Windows Live Spaces	109	1.8%	4
5	Flixster	90	1.5%	6
6	Friends Reunited	76	1.2%	5
7	WAYN	60	1.0%	21
8	Yahoo! Groups	59	1.0%	10
9	Faceparty	50	0.8%	17
10	BBC Communities	49	0.8%	6

Source: Nielsen Mobile, UK, Q1 2008.

Alex Burmaster, European Internet Analyst, Nielsen Online: 'The increasingly competitive nature of social networking online is being replicated in the mobile space. The leading players remain the same but networks such as WAYN and Faceparty have considerably improved on their PC ranking in the mobile world. In an effort to differentiate their offerings and pull ahead all the networks are looking to what the mobile medium can offer – particularly when it comes to attracting 15- to 24-year-olds, a group highly representative amongst social networking addicts.'

Most common mobile social-networking related activities

⇨ One in five (21%) Britons who use their mobile for social networking activities, use it to add friends.

Burmaster concludes, 'It's all about adding value. By tapping into the key elements of mobile phone activity, such as text and images, the social networks can increase engagement and "stickiness" amongst their members as well as maximising audience numbers and activity on their own site.

'For example, within minutes of a social networker making a new friend whilst out and about, they can add them to their digital friends list. This simultaneously enhances both the phone and the network as an extremely important modern-day social utility.'
12 May 2008

⇨ The above information is reprinted with kind permission from Nielsen Online. Visit www.nielsen-netratings.com for more information.
© Nielsen Online

Mobile Life Report 2008: the connected world

Exploring our relationships with modern technology in a wireless world

Technology behaviour: tech fix

If we needed more evidence that technology plays a crucial role in the lives of our two nations then we have it: TVs, computers and mobiles are almost universally

Currently, an average of 60% of adults both in the UK and in the US own one or more laptop computer and 88% have at least one desktop, meaning a fair few have both

owned in both the UK and US. For the younger generation, we can add games consoles and MP3 players to that list – in both cases three in every four young people in both the US and UK own or have access to them. One striking theme to emerge from the survey is that the British own more gadgets and this is true of almost every category. The most

stark difference is that 94% of British youngsters own mobile phones compared to 80% in the US.

Here's a tough question: What if we could only keep one of our devices?

Interestingly while adults said they would stick with their TV, youngsters on both sides of the pond consider their mobile phone to be their best friend. It is fascinating to see how far down the 'must-have' list the TV has dropped for most kids. As well as their mobile phone, our young US respondents are more likely to want to keep their computer than their TV. In the UK too, the TV is losing its significance with mobile phones, computers and games consoles all rated as more important.

The post-TV entertainment age seems to have well and truly arrived.

We also asked parents how they were most likely to punish their kids if they misbehaved and two of the most popular methods were to restrict TV or Internet use. Given our findings perhaps confiscating their mobile

phone for a few days might be more effective!

The rise of the laptop

Currently, an average of 60% of adults both in the UK and in the US own one or more laptop computer and 88% have at least one desktop, meaning a fair few have both. Perhaps the laptop will eventually take over; one quarter of desktop owners say they will swap their current desktop for a laptop when the time comes to replace it.

While the majority replace equipment when it becomes too slow or stops working altogether, 17% say they replace their IT equipment with the latest models as soon as they can afford to.

Mobile chat

When we look at how we use mobile phones, some interesting differences between the two nations emerge. While just 4% of British adults have resisted getting a mobile phone, in the US some 10% of adults are still mobile phone free. In fact, 17% of UK adults told us they owned two or more mobile phones compared to 11% in the US.

TVs, computers and mobiles are almost universally owned in both the UK and US

Similarly, the two countries use their mobile phones differently: broadly, Americans make more calls while the British send more texts.

More than a third of US youngsters and adults make six or more calls on an average day, while only 12% of UK kids and 16% of UK adults make this many calls. In fact, 22% of UK youngsters make no calls on an average day, compared to just 7% in the US.

By contrast, the majority of US adults do not send any texts on an average day, while over half their UK counterparts send between one and five texts per day and a further 31% send more than six.

British youth are really prolific texters, with 50% sending more than six every day. The most interesting point about the texting figures is the pattern for US kids – while they are much more likely than youngsters in the UK to send no texts on an average day (27% versus 9% in the UK) – they also make up the biggest group of heavy texters: 33% of US kids send 16+ texts a day. This points to the potential emergence of an interesting trend in the US: while SMS use has not really taken off amongst adults, perhaps the next generation are going to embrace texting with even more passion than young people in Britain.

Mobiles are the communication device of choice for youngsters in both countries, with more than half reporting that mobile calls and texts are their most important means of keeping in touch. Adults in the US largely favour email as the preferred communication with friends but in the UK there is an even split between texts and email.

Accessing the Internet via mobile phones

When we look at what people do online via their mobile phone, we find the generational divide is greater than the geographical one, with British youngsters leading the way. Amongst adults the only common online activity done via mobile phones is emailing (24% of US adults and 17% of UK adults have done this) followed by obtaining news or weather reports online via their mobile phone (14% in both countries). One in ten have also downloaded music or photos to their mobile phones.

With young people, the figures are much higher, especially for British teenagers. One in three British youngsters say they have accessed online gaming via their mobile and one in four have downloaded music or photos. Around one in six have sent emails or watched online videos via mobile phones. US kids are doing the same activities but in slightly lower numbers.

So while overall online activity from mobile phones remains limited, there are some signs of its increasing popularity on both sides of the Atlantic, in particular amongst the youth market.

Mobile must-haves

When considering what kind of mobile phone we want, adults and youngsters have very different demands. We asked people whether their ideal mobile phone:

1. MUST HAVE as many high-quality functions as possible, such as a camera, a portable radio and an Mp3 player;

2. WOULD BE GOOD IF IT HAD high-quality functions such as a camera, a portable radio and an Mp3 player;

3. Or if they would prefer it to be as SIMPLE AS POSSIBLE, and only include functions for talking, texting and pictures.

Youngsters in both countries wanted as many high-quality functions as possible (62% of UK kids and 46% in the US) while adults were more likely to opt for keeping it simple.

But, as we would expect from the more mature market, British adults are more technically demanding than their US counterparts. The majority of US adults plumped for keeping it simple and only 18% felt they needed the high-tech functions. For British adults there was indeed a preference for the simple option (38%), but 34% of British adults saw the functions as good to have while just over one quarter regarded high-tech functions as necessary.

It will be interesting to see how long it takes the next generation of mobile users in the US to catch up with this level of sophistication – we could speculate perhaps that the large group of heavy text users amongst younger people in the US represents a new generation of mobile phone users who will catch up with and perhaps even overtake the British demand for high-quality functions in the not-too-distant future.

The Internet: a tool for empowerment?

Nearly half of the US adults and more than a third of the British adults surveyed have Internet access at work but it appears that much of what we do online is not work-related. In both countries, only 50% of adults describe themselves as a heavy or moderate user of the Internet for work. In contrast, three-quarters of adults describe themselves as heavy or moderate Internet users for personal or leisure purposes.

Similarly while the Internet is revolutionising education, kids are actually more likely to be surfing than learning...

Around 95% of all youngsters use the Internet but it would seem that UK teenagers are more likely to have access to Internet at school than their American cousins (87% vs. 65%). They are therefore more likely to identify themselves as heavy or moderate users of the Internet for school or college work. But in both cases, a significant majority of youngsters (72% in UK and 68% in US) identify themselves as heavy or moderate users of the Internet for fun.

Internet confidence

When it comes to rating our confidence on the Internet, British youngsters are either the most highly skilled of the four groups, or perhaps just the cockiest! One in four British teenagers rate themselves as being so good that they say 'I know what I am doing and I don't need help.' Beyond this particularly confident group, there are over 50% of teenagers from both countries who rate themselves as 'quite good'.

When we look at what people do online via their mobile phone, we find the generational divide is greater than the geographical one

---

Adults in both countries are most likely to say 'I am ok but need help with things that are a bit different' while one in ten adults in both countries class themselves as beginners compared to just 3% of the youngsters. Again it is more of a generational divide than a geographic one. The geographical divide that is present between the young people, with British youngsters being the most confident could, as we saw earlier, be attributed to the greater access that British teenagers have to the Internet at school.

50% of American youngsters and 58% of their British counterparts think that they are more confident than their parents on computers and the Internet, but 66% of American parents and 61% of British parents think they are the more confident ones, perhaps illustrating that computers and the Internet are not something that families do together.

We asked adults who said they were less confident than their children how this made them feel and for the most part people said they were unbothered, although a minority – one in six – said they felt left behind.

We also asked adults how they felt when they were online. Half said being online came 'naturally' to them, while one in ten felt 'frustrated' and one in five felt 'amazed'!

Online activities

As we saw earlier, youngsters' online behaviour is largely driven by entertainment and for most activities there were few differences between young people in the two countries. Emailing friends was the most popular activity (88%), followed by watching videos (87%), visiting social networking sites (75%) and gaming (74%).

In addition, two-thirds are downloading and sharing photos online, half are shopping online and one in three have blogged. Clearly the next generation has a lot to say about themselves, and has a need to share it!

Again, it is British youngsters who tend to be the more sophisticated user, pursuing a greater range of activities online, whether it is communicating by webcam (something 53% of British youngsters have done compared to just 18% of their American cousins) or downloading films (33% of teenagers in the UK against 22% in the US). Skype is used by more than twice as many British young people, while chat rooms are favoured by 61% of teenagers in Britain compared to 47% in the US. Watching television online is favoured by 38% in the UK

and 27% in the US. It seems British kids are leading the way and these findings reveal a generation entirely comfortable with trying out a whole range of activities online in search of fun and entertainment.

Interestingly however, American teenagers are more likely to go online to look for factual information, maps and directions (56% of US teenagers versus 44% of British youngsters), and news and weather (63% of US teenagers versus 53% of British youngsters).

When it comes to adults' online behaviour, it is a rather less exciting picture with email (93%), maps and directions (89%), news and weather (88%) and shopping (86%) topping the list of activities on both sides of the Atlantic, with banking (75%) and paying bills (71%) not far behind.

However, it is not all drudgery and clearly some adults are also using the Internet for entertainment. Almost three-quarters have watched videos online, 67% have downloaded and shared photos, half use social networking sites or play video games online and the same number share music. One in three now even watch TV online.

⇨ The above information is an extract from the report *Mobile Life Report 2008: The Connected World*, and is reprinted with kind permission from the Carphone Warehouse. Visit www.www.mobilelife2008.co.uk for more information.

© Carphone Warehouse

What do Britons spend the most time doing online?

Instant Messaging, member communities sites and email account for the most time spent by Britons whilst surfing the web or using Internet-related applications

Nielsen Online, a global leader in Internet media and market research, today reveals where Britons are spending the most time whilst surfing the web and using Internet-related applications.

The 30.6 million Britons active online in June 2007 spent a total of 31.8 billion minutes surfing the web and using Internet-related applications

Categories where online Britons spend most of their time

⇨ The 30.6 million Britons active online in June 2007 spent a total of 31.8 billion minutes surfing the web and using Internet-related applications – an average of 17 hours 21 minutes per active Briton online.

⇨ Instant Messaging accounted for most of this time – 12.7% (3.4 billion minutes), followed by Member Communities – 9.4% (2.6 billion minutes).

⇨ The ten most engaging categories account for 42% of all time spent by Britons surfing the web and using Internet-related applications.

Alex Burmaster, European Internet Analyst, at Nielsen Online, comments, 'The online sectors where Britons spend most of their time highlights the power of the Internet as a tool to bring people closer together. Whether it's communicating via Instant Messaging and email or networking in communities, the Internet has an unrivalled ability to satisfy one of humankind's most basic needs – the need to connect.'

Within the top ten it's worth noting that the position of the 'Classifieds/ Auctions' category is entirely down to eBay. In fact, the huge amount of time Britons spend on eBay means that eBay, as a brand, racks up more total time than all but three of the 85 categories that NetRatings covers.

It's also worth noting that the popularity of a sector isn't necessarily aligned with how much total time it accounts for. Online Games, for example, is only the 26th most popular category but due to the highly engaging nature of playing games, it ranks as the fifth leading sector by total time. Its average time of 2 hours 13 minutes per visitor is surpassed only by Instant Messaging (3 hours 10 minutes per visitor) and Member Communities (2 hours 20 minutes per visitor).

26 July 2007

⇨ The above information is reprinted with kind permission from Nielsen Online. Visit www.nielsen-netratings.com for more information.

© Nielsen Online

What do we do online?

Categories accounting for the most time spent by UK internet population – June 2007

Rank	Category	% of total time	Total time (billions of minutes)	Time per person (hh:mm:ss)	Rank by unique audience
1	Instant Messaging	12.7%	3.4	3:10:00	6
2	Member Communities	9.4%	2.6	2:19:58	5
3	Email	7.8%	2.1	1:45:38	4
4	Classifieds/auctions	5.1%	1.4	1:33:46	12
5	Games	4.8%	1.3	2:12:55	26
6	Software manufacturers	4.4%	1.2	0:55:00	3
7	Search	4.2%	1.1	0:41:44	1
8	General interest portals & communities	3.7%	1.0	0:38:59	2
9	Multi-category entertainment	3.4%	0.9	0:54:21	9
10	Adult	2.6%	0.7	1:26:52	35

Source: Nielsen Online, NetView UK, home and work data, including applications, June 2007.

'Nerdic' is fastest-growing language

By Gary Cleland

From dongles to mashups to RickRolling, 'geek speak' has become the fastest-growing language in Europe as new words are invented to describe technological advances.

Experts claim about 100 new words are added to the language of technology, dubbed 'Nerdic', every year – three times the number of new words making it into the *Oxford English Dictionary*.

From dongles to mashups to RickRolling, 'geek speak' has become the fastest-growing language in Europe as new words are invented to describe technological advances

This year the number of new Nerdic words will rise to 200, according to research carried out by e-tailer pixmania.com to mark the 15th anniversary of the Internet.

Stuart Miles, the editor of gadget website Pocket-Lint.co.uk, said: 'Technology has revolutionised the way we speak. With so many words and phrases being created all the time it's created a whole new way of communicating.

'Everyone knows what it means to Google something, and technology is moving at such a rapid pace these days that there are more and more new words coming into the English language.

'Fifty years ago development was much slower and TVs were just a square box in the corner of the room, but now there's new technology every couple of months.'

He added: 'If you're really into technology like me, it is actually possible to have an entire conversation in Nerdic, although not everyone else would be able to understand it.'

Words created to describe technological breakthroughs can transcend other languages, the research found.

For example, the word 'Internet' is understood and used throughout the world, even in non-English-speaking countries.

In France, the translation of Internet is 'toile d'araignée mondiale' – but most people still refer to the Internet.

The word is also widely used in countries including Spain and Italy.

Now calls have even been made to have Nerdic recognised as an official language.

The researchers found that Nerdic contained the three core elements needed to define a language – words, phrases and pronunciation.

Ulric Jerome, the managing director of pixmania.com, said: 'Technology has infiltrated our lives

YOUTUBE FACEBOOK RICKROLL MASHUP WIMAX DONGLE FLICKR ANDROID

in many ways and at such a pace it is natural that it has developed a language of its own.

'It's exciting to see Nerdic bringing Europe together, and by recognising Nerdic as an official language the UK will continue to help unite technology fans across Europe.'

Pixmania.com's top 10 Nerdic words and phrases for 2008

1 Wimax – Supersized Wi-Fi will give whole cities Internet coverage, Milton Keynes already has it.

2 RickRoll – To intentionally misdirect Internet users to a video of Never Gonna Give You Up by 80s one-hit-wonder Rick Astley.

3 UGC (user generated content) – The buzz word in the Internet right now. Flickr, Facebook and YouTube all rely on the reader generating content on the sites.

4 Mashup – Take two or more really interesting elements from different websites or applications and make them into one – think Google Maps with an overlay of where you can buy clown outfits from.

5 RFID – Radio-frequency identification (RFID) will allow you to track your packages around the world or let you know how your bananas have travelled to you.

6 Android – Think iPhone but with a slightly different interface on phones from Samsung to HTC and with the ability for anyone to make applications for it.

7 HDMI – The new Scart lead allows you to connect High-Def devices together, like your TV to your new Blu-ray player.

8 Fuel-cell – Green water powered battery for everything from cars to laptops that will boost your gadget's life considerably over standard batteries.

9 HSDPA – The next step up from 3G on mobile phones. Makes accessing the Internet on your

mobile just as fast if not faster than your broadband connection at home.

10 DVB-H – Newly announced Mobile TV standard for Europe that allows you to watch TV on your mobile on the go.

Pixmania.com's top 10 Nerdic words to forget in 2008

1 HD DVD – Just like Betamax, HD DVD is now the dead format against Sony's Blu-ray in the HD disc battle when it comes to High-Def movies.

2 Dial-up – Broadband is the way to go if you are looking to surf the Internet so throw that 56k modem out with the garbage.

3 VHS – DVD players are so cheap and PVRs are so easy to use that the movie format that would take you 10 minutes to rewind after watching a film is dead.

4 Tri-band Replaced by Quad-band, 3G, or HSDPA to allow much better phone coverage abroad, much better for the traveller in you.

5 Hits – How website popularity used to be measured before people realise that unique visitors is what is important.

6 CRT – Fat TVs – flat is the new thin so get with the times and throw out your Fat TV.

7 KB – Standing for Kilobytes and important when computer

memory was a measly 64k. Look out for the new super-size Terabyte.

8 Floppy disk – Replaced by USB thumb drives and CDs the idea of only being able to get 1.4MB on a disk would now seem mad to the average 10-year-old.

9 MiniDisc – Sony's now defunct music format that was like the CD only smaller. Overtaken by MP3 before it even got going.

10 Super Audio CD – A higher quality CD format that never really took off. Why? Because you needed state-of-the-art expensive kit to run it on and there aren't enough audiophiles out there.

29 April 2008

Internet connectivity

Information from the Office for National Statistics

More than nine out of ten connections to the Internet are via broadband.

In March 2008, broadband connections accounted for 91.6 per cent of all Internet connections, up from 90 per cent in December 2007. This is according to the latest update from the survey of Internet Service Providers (ISPs). The index of all connections rose to 119.4 in March 2008, compared with the base month of March 2005. The index increased by 0.3 per cent between December 2007 and March 2008.

Dial-up connections continued to decline and accounted for 8.4 per cent of all Internet connections in March 2008.

Broadband and dial-up Internet connections

The market share of broadband connections has been increasing since the index began in 2001, reflecting its continuing popularity and widespread availability. ISPs have also been offering increasingly competitive connection packages.

In March 2008, the indices of active connections for dial-up and broadband were 19.7 and 222.6 respectively, when compared to their base of 100 in March 2005.

Broadband connections rose to 91.6 per cent of all connections in March 2008, up from 90 per cent in December 2007. There was a year-on-year increase in the index of broadband connections of 14.4 per cent, with a quarterly increase of 2.2 per cent.

In March 2008, broadband connections accounted for 91.6 per cent of all Internet connections, up from 90 per cent in December 2007

Dial-up connections continued to decrease, with a year-on-year fall in the index of 46.5 per cent to March 2008. The quarterly decrease, from December 2007 to March 2008, was 15.5 per cent.

Broadband connection speeds

As dial-up connections decrease, there is less interest in measuring the different types of dial-up, and more in broadband. Therefore, estimates on metered and unmetered dial-up

connections were discontinued from the December 2006 release. These have been replaced by estimates on broadband connection speed categories.

The speed advertised for each connection may not be the speed attained by the end user, as attained speed of connection is affected by issues such as distance from the local exchange and line quality.

As the proportion of slower speed connections has decreased, the proportion of higher speed connections has increased. In March 2008, 56.9 per cent of broadband connections had a speed greater than 2 Mbps, which is an increase from 51.2 per cent in December 2007 and 37.5 per cent in December 2006. Over the same period, the percentage of connections with a speed of less than or equal to 2 Mbps decreased to 43.1 per cent in March 2008, down from 48.7 per cent in December 2007 and 62 per cent in December 2006.

March 2008

⇨ The above information is reprinted with kind permission from the Office for National Statistics. Visit www.statistics.gov.uk for more information.

Government aims to bridge digital divide

Low-income families to be provided with PCs

By Neon Kelly

Reaching the least well-off is proving difficult for the government, which plans to give Internet access to the UK's most deprived areas.

The government is to spend £30m over the next three years to bring broadband access to schoolchildren and low-income families.

A further £600,000 has also been earmarked to subsidise home computers for entire year groups at 50 education institutions across the country, schools minister Jim Knight told an education conference last week.

The plan is the government's latest attempt to bridge the digital divide between those with access to technology and those without.

The government has already invested £5bn in IT for schools since 1997 and another £837m is budgeted over the next three years, according to Knight.

'We have the highest levels of embedded technology in classrooms in the European Union (EU) and one computer for every three pupils,' he said.

'The next step is home access for all – we have to find a way to make access universal, or it is not fair.'

The ubiquitous use of computers and the Internet is crucial to avoid reinforcing social and academic divisions. There is also a significant economic implication. Digital inclusion could be worth as much as £60bn to the EU economy over the next five years, according to the European Commission.

In the UK, 71 per cent of households have Internet access and 53 per cent have broadband. But reaching the least well-off is disproportionately difficult.

The government's plans are a step in the right direction but there is no easy answer, according to Association for Learning Technology (ALT) chief executive Seb Schmoller.

'Internet access in a developed economy must be a citizen's entitlement, like getting a drink of mains water,' said Schmoller. 'The challenge for the government is to bring it about.'

The main issue will concern connectivity.

'Remote areas are still out of reach of broadband, and connection costs remain stubbornly high,' said Schmoller.

'Poorer households often have no fixed line, nor the credit rating to obtain one, even if they can afford to pay.'

Alongside direct government subsidy, the competitive broadband market will target even the poorest homes, said Matt Yardley, principal consultant at telecoms researcher Analysys.

'If operators see an opportunity to tap unaddressed demand, perhaps through a lower cost offer with more constraints, they will go for it,' said Yardley.

'And those homes where people are avoiding line rental charges could well be targeted by mobile companies.'

Focusing on young people will also help, said Ovum analyst Mike Philpott.

'The number of broadband subscribers has grown rapidly, but the government recognises that the market will only drive uptake to a certain level,' he said.

'Getting kids online early means they will never go back, and they can also be used as an educational tool by teaching their parents.'

The 2008 ALT conference will discuss the digital divide in September.
17 January 2008

⇨ The above information is reprinted with kind permission from Computing. Visit www.computing.co.uk for more information.

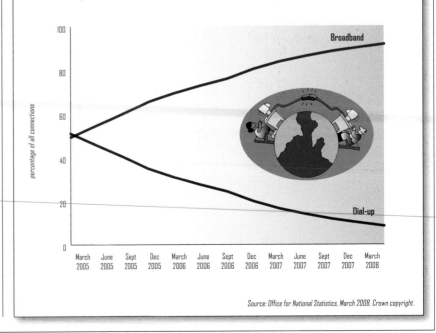

Internet connectivity

Indices of dial-up and broadband Internet connections, not seasonally adjusted.

percentage of all connections

Broadband

Dial-up

March 2005, June 2005, Sept 2005, Dec 2005, March 2006, June 2006, Sept 2006, Dec 2006, March 2007, June 2007, Sept 2007, Dec 2007, March 2008

Source: Office for National Statistics, March 2008. Crown copyright.

School work plagued by net plagiarism

Results of an ATL survey

the education union

Internet plagiarism is a major problem among sixth-form pupils according to over half the teachers questioned in an Association of Teachers and Lecturers (ATL) survey, out today.

Fifty-eight per cent of teachers said plagiarism is a problem. Of this group, 28 per cent estimated that half or more than half of work returned by their pupils included plagiarism. These findings come from an ATL survey on Internet plagiarism which questioned around 300 teachers working in school sixth forms, sixth-form colleges and further education colleges across England, Wales and Northern Ireland in December.

Some of the most blatant examples of plagiarism were:

Gill Bullen from Itchen College in Southampton said: 'Two GCSE English retake students were very late handing in their last piece of coursework, an essay on *Romeo and Juliet*. When finally given in, the pieces turned out to be identical – and significantly better than either of them could have done! Not only that, the essays given in didn't quite answer the title question I had set...'

A teacher from Leeds said: 'I had one piece of work so blatantly "cut + pasted" that it still contained adverts from the web page.'

ATL general secretary, Dr Mary Bousted, said: 'This survey highlights one of the risks of putting so much emphasis on passing tests and getting high scores at any cost. Unsurprisingly pupils are using all the means available to push up their coursework marks, often at the expense of any real understanding of the subjects they are studying.

'Long-term pupils are the real losers because they lack the skills they appear to have. And teachers are struggling under a mountain of cut and pasting to spot whether work was the student's own or plagiarism. Schools and colleges need to have robust policies to combat plagiarism, but they also need help from the exam boards and Government with resources and techniques for detecting cheating.'

For teachers plagiarism is a problem because it can be difficult to spot, and time consuming to have to continually check to see if students have copied work and presented it as their own.

Mark Jones, from Wirral Metropolitan College, said: 'Any work found to be plagiarised will not be marked – the student has to do it again. However, the problem is that, with the best will in the world, you haven't got enough hours in the day to search out where info was plagiarised from to prove it.'

Connie Robinson from Stockton Riverside College, Stockton on Tees, said: 'With less able students it is easy to spot plagiarism as the writing style changes mid assignment, but with more able students it is sometimes necessary for tutors to carry out Internet research to identify the source of the plagiarism – this obviously adds to the tutors' workloads.'

Teachers are also torn between wanting to ensure pupils are graded accurately and not wanting to put them at a disadvantage. A sixth-form teacher from Wiltshire summed up the dilemma: 'I am feeling a tension between wanting to be rigorous and not wanting to put my own students at a disadvantage when competing against other candidates whose teachers are not so scrupulous.'

Over 55 per cent of teachers said students don't have sufficient understanding of what is plagiarism and what counts as legitimate research.

Diana Baker from Emmanuel College in Durham said: 'I have found once students clearly understand what plagiarism is, its consequences and how to reference correctly so they can draw on published works, plagiarism becomes less of a problem. I think the majority of students who engage in plagiarism do it more out of ignorance than the desire to cheat, they really want to succeed on their own merit.'

Having a robust school or college policy on plagiarism seems to be critical. But over 55 per cent said either their school doesn't have a policy to deal with plagiarism or they are unaware of one.

Teachers are concerned about the continued use of course work in A levels. A teacher from East London said: 'The new A-level syllabuses are going to make this a far, far more serious problem with the emphasis more on coursework.'

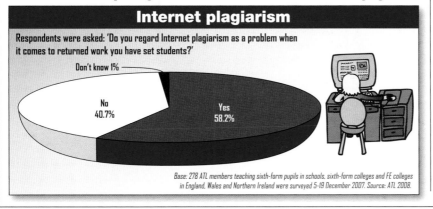

Internet plagiarism

Respondents were asked: 'Do you regard Internet plagiarism as a problem when it comes to returned work you have set students?'

Don't know 1%

No 40.7%

Yes 58.2%

Base: 278 ATL members teaching sixth-form pupils in schools, sixth-form colleges and FE colleges in England, Wales and Northern Ireland were surveyed 5-19 December 2007. Source: ATL 2008.

A sixth-form teacher from Wiltshire said: 'I am Head of English and have moved over the years from being a firm supporter of coursework to wishing it would disappear entirely. I am depressed that English remains one of the only subjects to retain it in the new syllabi.'

And over 90 per cent of teachers are concerned about the impact of plagiarism on their students' long-term prospects.

Beverley Alaimo, from Newcastle-under-Lyme College in Staffordshire, said: 'I believe students who provide excellent pieces of work which achieve a high grade will find progression to a higher level far more difficult, as they will not have the knowledge and understanding necessary to cope with the work, however, new lecturers will, again, assume that students do.'
18 January 2008

⇨ The above information is reprinted with kind permission from the Association of Teachers and Lecturers. Visit www.atl.org.uk for more information.

© *ATL*

Time to trust the digital generation says think tank

Schools and parents need to stop listening to Internet myths to help children get the best out of technology

In a report launched today (Thursday) the influential think tank Demos calls on schools to get past fears about children's Internet use and harness its learning potential. The report *Their Space: Education for a digital generation* draws on research showing that a generation of children have made online activity a part of everyday life, with parents and schools still far behind.

The report argues that children are developing a sophisticated understanding of new technologies outside of formal schooling, gaining creative and entrepreneurial skills demanded by the global knowledge economy. Schools are failing to develop these skills, with many attempting to limit children's online activity to ICT 'ghettos' while banning the use of social networking sites like MySpace and YouTube.

The research, based on nine months of interviews, focus groups and recording children's online activity, found that:

⇨ A majority of children use new media tools to make their lives easier and strengthen existing friendship networks.

⇨ Almost all children involved in creative production – e.g. uploading/editing photos and building websites.

⇨ A smaller group of 'digital pioneers' are engaged in more groundbreaking activities.

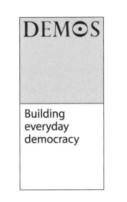

DEMOS

Building everyday democracy

⇨ Children are well aware of potential risks, with many able to self-regulate – contrary to popular assumptions about safety.

⇨ Many children have their own 'hierarchy of digital activity' and are much more conscious of the relative values of online activity than their parents and teachers.

Head of the Demos families programme, Hannah Green, said:

'We are witnessing the rise of a generation of children who can't remember life before the Internet and mobile phones. Negative myths are clouding the public debate around technology and children, and we rarely listen to what children themselves have to say. They know more than we think about what benefits them and what doesn't. It's time for schools to harness their knowledge and enthusiasm and start helping children who are less confident to contribute to a thriving digital culture.'

The report makes a number of proposals on how formal education can adapt to the growing dominance of online culture in children's lives:

- The Children's Commissioner should convene a working group of children to advise on children's use of technology.
- The development of a national strategy, led by schools in combating the 'digital divide', with schools responsible for delivering access to hardware such as a laptop, tablet or mobile device for every child.
- Measures should be taken to tackle a divide in knowledge, with schools working with parents to develop the skills to help all children interact with technology confidently and safely.
- Children should be given the opportunity to build up a 'creative portfolio' alongside traditional forms of assessment, access to which would be determined by the children themselves.

Notes

- *TheirSpace: Education for a digital generation* by Hannah Green and Celia Hannon will be launched on Thursday at the Bett 2007 educational technology show. Preview PDF copies are available on request.
- Hannah Green is head of the Demos families programme, and Celia Hannon is a researcher at Demos.
- The research and report are supported by the National College for Schools Leadership.
- The research took place between April and December 2006 and included:
- Seminars with senior policy makers, academics, head teachers and commentators.
- Expert interviews.

- Six months of interviews and group discussion with children around the UK.
- Diaries kept by children recording new media consumption – what they used, what they used it for, and how often.
- Poll of 600 parents on their views and understanding of children's digital technology use .
- Demos is the think tank for everyday democracy, the idea that all people should have greater influence over factors that affect them and their communities.

11 January 2007

- The above information is reprinted with kind permission from Demos. Visit www.demos.co.uk for more information on this and other topics.

© Demos

Online TV, video and movie consumption almost doubles

Over the last year the numbers of Britons visiting TV, video and movie sites is up 28%; the total UK time spent on these sites up 91%

Nielsen Online, a service of The Nielsen Company, today reveals the increasing degree to which Britons are using the Internet for TV, video and movie content.
- Almost 21 million Britons visited a TV, video or movie-related website in Sept 2007 – a 28% increase in visitors since Sept 2006.

- The TV/Video/Movie sector online is now visited by 63% of Britons online; up from 55% in Sept 2006 – a growth rate of 15%.
- The total time Britons spend consuming content from TV/Video/Movie sites almost doubles – increasing 91% from 641 million

minutes in Sept 2006 to 1.2 billion minutes in Sept 2007.

Alex Burmaster, Internet Analyst, Nielsen Online, comments 'Britons are displaying an increasingly significant appetite for supplementing their viewing habits online. Whether it's additional content relating to a particular TV programme or actually watching episodes or videos through their computer, we are starting to see a significant spread of entertainment consumption from the so-called "lean-back" method of TV to the "lean-forward" method of the PC.'

The most popular TV, video and movie websites
- YouTube is the most popular and most engaging TV, video or movie site being visited by 9.4 million Britons who spend a combined total of almost half a billion minutes on the site.
- The top ten contain four major broadcasters, two social media

TV, video and movie content online

Growth of TV/video/movie sector* – UK, September 2006-07.

TV/video/movie sector	September 2006	September 2007	% growth
Unique UK audience (millions)	16.3	20.8	+28%
UK active reach	55%	63%	+15%
Total UK minutes (millions)	641	1,223	+91%

* 'TV/video/movie' sector is a custom category compiled by the Nielsen Online PR team.

Source: Nielsen Online, UK NetView, home and work data, including applications, September 2006-07.

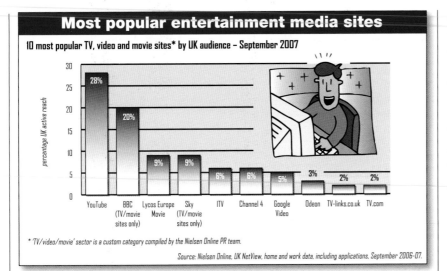

Most popular entertainment media sites

10 most popular TV, video and movie sites* by UK audience – September 2007

percentage UK active reach

Site	%
YouTube	28%
BBC (TV/movie sites only)	20%
Lycos Europe Movie	9%
Sky (TV/movie sites only)	9%
ITV	6%
Channel 4	6%
Google Video	5%
Odeon	3%
TV-links.co.uk	2%
TV.com	2%

* 'TV/video/movie' sector is a custom category compiled by the Nielsen Online PR team.

Source: Nielsen Online, UK NetView, home and work data, including applications, September 2006-07.

video sites, two movie information sites and two sites for general TV content.

'The fact that YouTube is the most popular site in this sector shows the power of social media as an entertainment form – and the threat or opportunity it poses for traditional media players, depending on your point of view. It's also interesting to note that TV-links.co.uk – the ninth most popular site and, amongst the top ten, second only to YouTube in terms of total audience time – has now been closed after claims it was illegally providing links to download film content and TV shows.

'Whilst the legality of the site is in question, the appetite that people have for watching this type of content online isn't. It is an example of the potential audiences that await media content owners – particularly when it comes to back catalogues – if they can just get their content up and available online.'
6 November 2007

⇨ The above information is reprinted with kind permission from Nielsen Online. Visit www.nielsen-netratings.com for more information.

© Nielsen Online

Microsoft to get touchy with next OS

The next version of its Windows operating system will have touch-screen controls, Microsoft has claimed

Microsoft plans to give users of the next version of its Windows operating system touch-screen controls as one option for controlling the software, its top executives said.

Chairman Bill Gates and chief executive Steve Ballmer showed off new Windows features based on software it calls 'multi-touch' that will be part of Windows 7, the next version of Windows, which Ballmer said was due out in late 2009.

The ability to use touch to give users fingertip control of their screens could help revolutionise how computer desktops and mobile phones are controlled and would be an alternative to existing mice, keyboard and pen-based user controls.

During a joint interview that kicked off the *Wall Street Journal*'s three-day D: All Things Digital conference, an annual gathering of the computer industry elite taking place north of San Diego, Ballmer said touch-screen controls was one example of how Microsoft would improve on existing Windows software.

> **Microsoft plans to give users of the next version of its Windows operating system touch-screen controls as one option for controlling the software**

Microsoft is seeking to one-up Apple Inc, which made touch-screen software central to the success of its iPhone mobile device, which combines computer, phone and web features and has sold around six million units in its first 11 months.

After more than a decade of slow development, Gates said new ways of interacting with computers other than keyboards and mice have matured to the point where they are ready to go mainstream.

'We are at an interesting juncture where almost all of the interaction is with the computer and mouse, today, and, over the years to come, the role of speech, vision, ink, all of those will become huge,' Gates said.

He was referring to technologies that give users the ability to control computers with voice commands, detect and sort different kinds of images and use electronic ink instead of typing for computer input.

Multi-touch software builds on existing capabilities Microsoft has introduced in recent years including Surface, for interacting with large tabletop computer displays, TouchWall for mounted screens and Tablet PCs for touch-screen notebooks.

In a demonstration of touch-screen capabilities to be offered in Windows 7, Microsoft showed a new application called 'Touchable Paint' that lets a user paint with their fingers, as well as software to organise photos or navigate maps by touch.

'It is not about complete replacement of the mouse,' Julie Larson-Green, Microsoft's corporate vice president in charge of Windows Experience Program Management, said in a first-time demonstration of multi-touch features to run inside Windows 7.

Ballmer said Microsoft is trying to learn from the reaction to Windows Vista, the latest version of its operating system, which was introduced in January 2007 but faced initial criticism for being incompatible with many older applications.

He said Microsoft has sold 150 million copies of Vista, up from 140 million the company reported it had sold a month ago.

'When you read the customer research, the No.1 people found jarring is that we changed the user interface,' Ballmer said. 'People take a while to get used to it.'

He said Microsoft had learned lessons about making dramatic changes in the way users interact with new versions of Windows. Conference co-host Walter Mossberg asked Ballmer whether Microsoft was done changing the user interface.

'We will polish it,' Ballmer replied. 'We will change it, but there are ways to change it and there are times to do it.'

Vista followed five years after the previous Windows upgrade and was beset by delays due to the complexity of updating a piece of software with some 50 million lines of code that runs on more than 90 per cent of the world's computers.

After the problems of releasing Vista in a timely manner, Ballmer pledged to never again wait so long between releases of its Windows operating system. Microsoft has said it expected to release the new operating system code-named Windows 7 around three years after the early 2007 release of Windows Vista.

Ballmer acknowledged that Microsoft considered Apple a formidable competitor. But he said the two companies' audiences were vastly different in scale, with Apple supplying around 10 million computers this year versus the roughly 290 million machines which PC makers will sell running Microsoft Windows.

'Whether Apple has a PC with touch in it to market first, we'll see,' Ballmer said.
28 May 2008

⇨ Copyright 2008 Reuters. Reprinted with permission from Reuters. Reuters content is the intellectual property of Reuters or its third party content providers. Any copying, republication or re-distribution of Reuters content is expressly prohibited without the prior written consent of Reuters. Reuters shall not be liable for any errors or delays in content, or for any actions taken in reliance thereon. Reuters and the Reuters Sphere Logo are registered trademarks of the Reuters group of companies around the world. For additional information about Reuters content and services, please visit Reuters website at www.reuters.com. Licence # REU-4176-JJM.

© Reuters

Gates convinced speech will replace keyboards

Within five years, more Internet searches will be conducted using speech recognition than a keyboard, claims Bill Gates

Speaking to staff and students at Carnegie Mellon University, Gates reiterated his long-stated belief that computer users will soon be abandoning their keyboards in favour of speech recognition and touchscreen technologies.

The development of new interface technologies has been a common theme of Gates' over the years, though his predictions have so far proved somewhat ambitious.

'In this 10-year time frame, I believe we will have perfected speech recognition and speech output well enough that those will become a standard part of the interface,' he said during a keynote in 1997.

However, speaking at Carnegie Mellon he went on to describe the development of speech and touch technology as 'one of the big bets we're making,' referring initially to Microsoft's rollout of Surface technology last year.

Surface comprises of a 30in touchscreen laid horizontally as a table top. The device is expected to sell for between $5,000 and $10,000, although cheaper consumer models are in development.

Gates is due to step down from day-to-day work at Microsoft in July 2008, although he will remain in position as chairman. Gates' talk at Carnegie Mellon was part of his final tour of speeches before the transition.

By Matthew Sparkes
25 February 2008

⇨ The above information is reprinted with kind permission from PC Pro. Visit www.pcpro.co.uk for more information.

© PC Pro

Internet 'to hit full capacity by 2010'

Information from ZDNet

By Andrew Donoghue

The US telecoms giant AT&T has claimed that, without investment, the Internet's current network architecture will reach the limits of its capacity by 2010.

Speaking at a Westminster eForum on Web 2.0 this week in London, Jim Cicconi, vice president of legislative affairs for AT&T, warned that the current systems that constitute the Internet will not be able to cope with the increasing amounts of video and user-generated content being uploaded.

'The surge in online content is at the centre of the most dramatic changes affecting the Internet today,' he said. 'In three years' time 20 typical households here in London will generate more traffic than the entire Internet did back in 1995.'

Cicconi, who was speaking at the event as part of a wider series of meetings with UK government officials, said that at least $55bn (£27.5bn) worth of investment was needed in new infrastructure in the next three years in the US alone, with the figure rising to $130bn to improve the network worldwide. 'We are going to be butting up against the physical capacity of the Internet by 2010,' he said.

He claimed that the 'unprecedented new wave of broadband traffic' would increase fiftyfold by 2015 and that AT&T was investing $19bn to maintain its network and upgrade its backbone network.

Cicconi added that more demand for high-definition (HD) video will put increasing strain on the Internet infrastructure. 'Eight hours of video is loaded onto YouTube every minute. Everything will become HD very soon and HD is seven to 10 times more bandwidth-hungry than typical video today. Video will be 80 per cent of all traffic by 2010, up from 30 per cent today,' he said.

The AT&T executive pointed out that the Internet only exists thanks to the infrastructure provided by a group of mostly private companies. 'There is nothing magic or ethereal about the Internet – it is no more ethereal than the highway system. It is not created by an act of God but upgraded and maintained by private investors,' he said.

> **'In three years' time 20 typical households here in London will generate more traffic than the entire Internet did back in 1995'**

Although Cicconi's speech did not explicitly refer to the term 'net neutrality', some audience members tackled him on the issue in a question-and-answer session, asking whether the subtext of his speech was really around prioritising some kinds of traffic. Cicconi responded by saying he believed government intervention in the Internet was fundamentally wrong.

'I think people agree why the Internet is successful. My personal view is that government has widely chosen to... keep a light touch and let innovators develop it,' he said. 'The reason I resist using the term "net neutrality" is that I don't think government intervention is the right way to do this kind of thing. I don't think government can anticipate these kinds of technical problems. Right now I think net neutrality is a solution in search of a problem.'

Net neutrality refers to an ongoing campaign calling for governments to legislate to prevent Internet service providers (ISPs) from charging content providers for prioritisation of their traffic. The debate is more heated in the US than in the UK because there is less competition between ISPs in the US.

Content creators argue that net neutrality should be legislated for in order to protect consumers and keep all Internet traffic equal. Network operators and service providers argue that the Internet is already unequal and certain types of traffic – VoIP, for example – require prioritisation by default.

'However well-intentioned, regulatory restraints can inefficiently skew investment, delay innovation and diminish consumer welfare, and there is reason to believe that the kinds of broad marketplace restrictions proposed in the name of "neutrality" would do just that with respect to the Internet,' the US Department of Justice said in a statement last year.

The BBC has come under fire from service providers, such as Tiscali, which claim that its iPlayer online-TV service is becoming a major drain on network bandwidth. In a recent posting on his BBC blog, Ashley Highfield, the corporation's director of future media and technology, defended the iPlayer: 'I would not suggest that ISPs start to try and charge content providers. They are already charging their customers for broadband to receive any content they want.'
18 April 2008

Tim Berners-Lee: The web that thinks

The groundwork is being laid for an intelligent web that will understand links and anticipate needs, says Claudine Beaumont

How will the Internet look in five years' time? According to Sir Tim Berners-Lee, the man credited with inventing the world wide web, it will be rather different to the cyberspace of today. He envisages an Internet in which all information, applications and data are seamlessly linked and interwoven – everything will work with everything else and that will, in effect, allow us to live our lives almost entirely online.

Technology experts call this the 'semantic web'. At the moment, search engines such as Google place more emphasis on the links and connections between websites, rather than on analysing the specific information contained within them. The semantic web, by contrast, will focus on the meaning of data on a page.

Computers will 'understand' the context of information and will be able to identify and appreciate the complex links between people, places and data, pulling it together to deliver rich search results and a better online experience.

'The semantic web is not a separate web but an extension of the current one,' said Berners-Lee. 'Information is given well-defined meaning, better enabling computers and people to work in cooperation.'

Tim Berners-Lee envisages an Internet in which all information, applications and data are seamlessly linked and interwoven

---

He recently explained how the semantic web could help people to track their finances. He gave the example of an online bank statement and a personal calendar, in which by dragging and dropping the information from the calendar on to the statement you could identify the periods of high expenditure.

He also said that could be taken one stage further by pulling digital photo albums into the mix, tallying pictures of family days out with spending peaks on the bank statement. This would be a seamless, behind-the-scenes process; web users would only see the end result, rather than how it was achieved.

The idea of the semantic web is gaining a lot of backing from forward-thinking technology start-ups as well as already established companies. Last week Yahoo!, the subject of a hostile takeover bid from Microsoft, announced that it would be building principles of the semantic web into its search engine and adopting some of the key 'standards' – rules about categorising and tagging information that will standardise the way data is organised – when indexing information on the Internet.

These standards are crucial, as they provide a simple and consistent way to easily add relevant context to data.

Most current search engines are unable to 'read' some of the information found on the Internet that might be relevant to a search enquiry, such as videos or photos, because they haven't been tagged with consistent 'metadata', the labels that tell computers what a piece of data means.

'While there has been remarkable progress made toward understanding the semantics of web content, the benefits of a data web have not reached the mainstream consumer,' said Amit Kumar, Yahoo!'s director of project management. 'Without a killer semantic web application for consumers, site owners have been reluctant to support standards.'

Yahoo! hopes that by indexing semantically tagged pages, it will encourage website owners to invest more time in the process of attaching

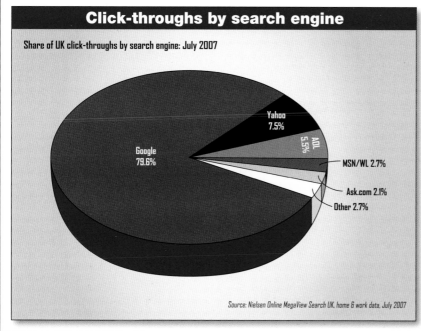

Click-throughs by search engine

Share of UK click-throughs by search engine: July 2007

Google 79.6%
Yahoo 7.5%
AOL 5.5%
MSN/WL 2.7%
Ask.com 2.1%
Other 2.7%

Source: Nielsen Online MegaView Search UK, home & work data, July 2007

standardised metadata to all the information they put on their sites. This should ensure a higher ranking and greater exposure in Yahoo! search results.

Moving towards a semantic web does not mean ripping up the Internet and starting again

'By supporting semantic web standards, Yahoo! search and site owners can create a far richer and more useful search experience for consumers,' said Kumar.

For example, if you searched Yahoo!'s semantics-based search engine for information about a film star, it would understand the context of the enquiry and pull together a wealth of information from across the Internet.

You might get a biography of the actor, links to film reviews, the option to rent his back catalogue from an online video store, local cinema details and the option to book cinema tickets, information about other actors he has worked with, as well as recent news stories, video footage of interviews and film trailers. What might currently take two or three separate Internet searches to produce will in future only take one.

However, as technology commentator Paul Miller points out, moving towards a semantic web does not mean ripping up the Internet and starting again.

'Despite the hype, not everything about the semantic web has to be paradigm shifting and revolutionary,' he said. 'Many of the benefits will simply come as existing systems become more open and as existing data moves a little more freely and purposefully.'

Nova Spivack is an entrepreneur and Internet visionary who has invested time and energy into making the semantic web a reality. He runs a website called Twine (twine. com), a virtual network currently in invitation-only beta testing that is designed to enable people to discover, organise and share information, and form new connections.

Spivack believes that services such as Twine will be crucial to enabling people to make sense of this new intelligent web, by providing the tools by which they can turn semantic web content into a useful, personalised information repository.

By building a network of interconnected and richly realised information, services such as Twine will help people to find things they didn't even know they were looking for.

'I believe Yahoo!'s announcement marks the beginning of the mainstream semantic web,' Spivack wrote on his blog.

'It should quickly catalyse an arms race by search engines, advertisers and content providers to make the best use of semantic metadata on the web. This will benefit the entire semantic sector and all players in it. As they say, "a rising tide lifts all boats".'

He's right – it's likely that other Internet companies will be spurred into action by Yahoo!'s backing for the semantic web, racing to bring their own semantic offerings to market.

Some detractors, however, fear the semantic web may never realise its full potential, because it relies so heavily on companies – in many cases, direct competitors – working together, cooperating, agreeing on common standards and sticking to them.

The spirit of openness that the semantic web fosters is perhaps anathema to many big technology organisations, who until now have jealously guarded their platforms and software and may be reluctant to break down those barriers in order to benefit consumers.

But it is likely that most search engines will see the semantic web as adding value to what they already do – if another search platform or product can develop a service that is more useful and more compelling than that offered by the dominant search engine, Google, then users will soon follow. So will advertisers and, with them, the licence to print money.

Welcome to the future.

20 March 2008

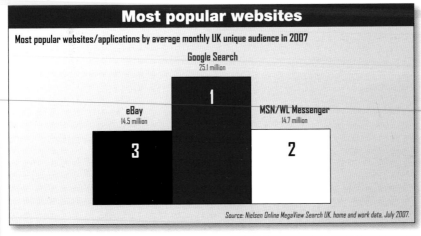

Most popular websites

Most popular websites/applications by average monthly UK unique audience in 2007

Google Search
25.1 million

1

eBay
14.5 million

3

MSN/WL Messenger
14.7 million

2

Source: Nielsen Online MegaView Search UK, home and work data. July 2007.

A generation of youth are being 'raised online'

Information from the Institute for Public Policy Research

Many young people are effectively being 'raised online' spending in excess of 20 hours a week using sites such as Bebo, MySpace, Facebook and YouTube, according to new research to be published by the Institute for Public Policy Research (ippr) next month. This is over three times higher than previous official estimates. This new research comes ahead of the final report of the Byron Review of children and new technology, set up by Gordon Brown in 2007 and headed by Dr Tanya Byron.

Young people are spending in excess of 20 hours a week using sites such as Bebo, MySpace, Facebook and YouTube

---

ippr worked with young people aged between 13 and 18, holding deliberative workshops and in-depth interviews. The research found that young people are 'constantly connected' staying up to the early hours with many leaving their mobile phones on all night in case they receive a text message. But a lack of parental knowledge and understanding means that few have any idea about what their children are doing online.

The report argues that with children being 'raised online' the Government and Internet companies need to do more to protect young people from inappropriate content and to promote and enforce guidelines on the limits of acceptable behaviour. ippr's report will recommend that:

⇨ Ofcom should produce an annual report on the effectiveness of initiatives aimed at tackling harmful Internet content. It should make recommendations to Government where gaps exist (for example, in tackling violent user-generated content online) and where industry should be taking further action. If industry does not make progress in this area, the Government should consider extending Ofcom's remit to cover Internet content.

⇨ Sites popular with young people, for example MySpace, Bebo and YouTube, should develop cross-industry guidelines setting out the limits of what young people can expect and how young people are expected to behave in return. Ofcom should approve this and ensure sites are enforcing these guidelines.

⇨ Such sites should commit to existing schemes to keep young people safe online for instance by becoming funding members of the Internet Watch Foundation.

⇨ The Department for Children, Schools and Families (DCFS) should be given overall control for media literacy. Information and support for parents should be provided through the extended schools programme and available through initiatives such as Sure Start; so that parents can make sure their children get the best out of the Internet without being exposed to unnecessary risks.

Kay Withers, ippr research fellow and report author, said:

'The Internet offers great benefits and opportunities for young people. But with kids spending an ever increasing amount of time online parents need to be reassured about what they are looking at. Government needs to improve media literacy programmes for kids and to make sure parents are aware of how they can support young people's positive online experiences. But more importantly Internet companies need to take more responsibility for the content on their sites and promote acceptable behaviour.'
24 March 2008

⇨ The above information is reprinted with kind permission from the Institute for Public Policy Research. Visit www.ippr.org.uk for more information.
© IPPR

'My mum will ask sometimes "is it safe?" but she doesn't really know' (Girl, 16, ABC1)

'Everyone lies about their age 'cos I think it's like if you're under 18, your profile gets set to private' (Girl, 15)

'We have restrictions at school but we can just get an administrator's account and take them off' (Boy, 14)

'Restrictions stop you going on bad sites, like games sites and stuff. If you take them off you can go on anything' (Boy, 14)

'I want to spend less time 'cos what I do on it is just really pointless – like MySpace is just really addictive' (Girl, 17)

'First it was like everyone was on MSN, then everyone sort of has Bebo, now everyone who had MSN moved on to Facebook so it's just what everyone's doing at that time' (Girl, 16)

'Some things they [parents] don't understand and they ask me to explain it to them but they still don't understand' (Girl, 13)

UK kids take online risks behind closed doors

Information from Garlik

Children's illicit online activity is putting them in danger, with parents totally oblivious to this high-risk behaviour according to new research published today.

The report from online identity experts Garlik reveals that one in five young people in Britain has met up with someone first encountered online and a further one in twenty does so on a regular basis. Yet, only seven per cent of parents are aware that their children are doing this.

The Garlik research which questioned 8- to 15-year-olds and parents across the UK goes on to reveal that four in ten young people regularly visit websites that are specifically prohibited by their parents and many hand out sensitive personal information without parental consent. Details divulged include full name (30 per cent), home address (12 per cent), mobile number (20 per cent), home telephone number (10 per cent), school details (46 per cent) and family photos (9 per cent).

As a result one in ten (11 per cent) young people have been cyber bullied – with victims intimidated by email or on chat-rooms – yet only half have spoken to their parents about their ordeals, with girls more likely than boys to keep schtum.

And it's no wonder parents are kept in the dark. Despite nine in ten monitoring their offspring's Internet activities more than half of the 8- to 15-years-olds questioned admitted to surfing the Internet when their parents didn't know, often late at night.

While the majority of online activity undertaken includes playing games (74 per cent), researching homework (66 per cent) and chatting with people they know in 'real life' (65 per cent), one in five chats with 'friends' they've only met online and one in twenty meets and chats with strangers.

Tom Ilube, CEO, Garlik said: 'Our research is a shocking wake-up call to all parents in the UK to sit down with their children and talk about how to keep safe online. The Web is a wonderful place to explore but young people continue to make themselves vulnerable by not applying the same caution online as they would in person.'

Garlik is hosting a live web cast chaired by ITV's "This Morning" presenter Paul Ross with among the panellists John Carr of children's charity NCH, on Monday 4 June at 9pm to discuss children's safety online.

Ilube continued: 'It's important for parents to understand the risks their children could face when on the net and whether their children are behaving responsibly. At Garlik we want to help people take control and protect their privacy online, but also understand the steps to protecting their families too.'

To take part in the live web cast or for more advice on how to keep your children safe online visit www. garlik.com.

31 May 2007

Garlik's top tips for parents

1 Keep Internet-connected computers in a central and open location, particularly for younger children.
2 Sit down and talk to your children about their online activity. You should know everyone on your children's contact list.
3 For younger kids, make sure you know all their passwords. Don't intrude, but let them know that you know, just in case.
4 Tell your children not to provide personal details online. No full names, addresses or telephone numbers.
5 Devise a code of conduct – list of Internet rules – that you and your children agree to sign up to.

⇨ The above information is reprinted with kind permission from Garlik. Visit www.garlik.com for more.
© Garlik

Safer children in a digital world

Byron Review urges government, industry and parents to work together to help make children safer in the digital world

A comprehensive package of measures to help children and young people make the most of the Internet and video games, while protecting them from harmful and inappropriate material, was launched today with the publication of the eagerly anticipated Byron Review into Children and New Technology.

In launching her independent Report today, *Safer Children in a Digital World*, Dr Tanya Byron, a clinical psychologist and mother of two, set out an ambitious action plan for Government, industry and families to work together to support children's safety online and to reduce access to adult video games.

Since being asked by the Prime Minister in September 2007 to lead an independent review, Dr Byron has engaged in a rigorous process and has been widely complimented for setting new standards in engagement with the public and industry on such an important debate. As a result of these efforts, Dr Byron has been able to set out a detailed analysis of the evidence of the risks and benefits of new technologies, examine this evidence against child and brain development theory and research and provide a comprehensive evaluation of the work already being done to protect children when they are online or playing video games.

While new technologies bring incredible opportunities to young people, parents' general lack of confidence and awareness is leaving children vulnerable to risks within their digital worlds

---

Dr Byron concludes that while new technologies bring incredible opportunities to children and young people, parents' general lack of confidence and awareness is leaving children vulnerable to risks within their digital worlds. Many parents seem to believe that when their child is online it is similar to watching television. Dr Byron is keen to emphasise that in fact it is more like opening the front door and letting a child go outside to play, unsupervised. Digital world risks are similar to real world risks but can be enhanced by the anonymity and ubiquity that the online space brings.

In order to improve children's online safety, Dr Byron makes a number of groundbreaking recommendations including:

⇨ The creation of a new UK Council for Child Internet Safety, established by and reporting to the Prime Minister, and including representation from across Government, industry, children's charities and other key stakeholders including children, young people and parent panels.

⇨ Challenging industry to take greater responsibility in supporting families through: establishing transparent and independently monitored codes of practice on areas such as user-generated content; improving access to parental control software and safe search features; and better regulation of online advertising.

⇨ Kick-starting a comprehensive public information and awareness campaign on child Internet safety across Government and industry, which includes an authoritative 'one stop shop' on child Internet safety.

⇨ Setting in place sustainable education and initiatives in children's services and education to improve the skills of children and their parents around e-safety.

On video games, Dr Byron recommends a range of high profile and targeted efforts to help inform parents what games are right for their children, such as:

⇨ Reforming the classification

system for rating video games with one set of symbols on the front of all boxes which are the same as those for film.

⇨ Lowering the statutory requirement to classify video games to 12+, so that it is the same as film classification and easier for parents to understand.

⇨ Clear and consistent guidance for industry on how games should be advertised.

⇨ Challenging industry to provide sustained and high profile efforts to increase parents' understanding of age ratings and improved parental controls.

Dr Byron said:

'The Internet and video games are now very much a part of growing up and offer unprecedented opportunities to learn, develop and have fun. However, with new opportunities come potential risks. My recommendations will help children and young people make the most of what all digital and interactive technologies can offer, while enabling them and their parents to navigate all these new media waters safely and with the knowledge that more is being done by government and the Internet and video game industries to help and support them.

'We live in an increasingly risk-averse culture where we are limiting our children's out-of-home experiences because of fear of harm. However, risk taking is a developmental imperative of childhood – young people and children will always want to explore boundaries by taking risks, and they will sometimes play this out, at home, in the digital world with many parents unaware of this. In the same way that we teach our children how to manage "real world" risks, for example crossing roads, in stages and with rules, supervision and monitoring that changes as they learn and develop their independence, we need to engage with children as they develop and explore their online and gaming worlds.

'This is also about overcoming the generational "digital divide" where parents do not feel equipped to help their children because they didn't grow up with these sophisticated technologies themselves and therefore don't understand them; this can lead to fear and a sense of helplessness. This is compounded by children and young people's greater skill and confidence in using new technology.

'But by putting in place the right roles and support for children, young people and families we can reduce much of the anxiety that currently exists by taking a joint and shared responsibility, with everyone – industries, Government, education, child welfare organisations and law enforcement – playing their part.

'A useful way for us all to think about this is to look at how we protect children in places of benefit and risk in the real (offline) world: public swimming pools. Here there are safety signs and information; shallow as well as deep ends; swimming aids and lifeguards; doors, locks and alarms. However, children will sometimes take risks and jump into waters too deep for them or want to climb walls and get through locked doors – therefore we also teach them how to swim. We must adopt the same combination of approaches in order to enable our children and young people to navigate these exciting digital waters while supporting and empowering them to do so safely.'
27 March 2008

⇨ The above information is reprinted with kind permission from the Department for Children, Schools and Families. Visit www.dcsf.gov.uk for more information.
© Crown copyright

Online shopping reaches record high

Information from Silicon.com

Online shopping jumped in January, with sales reaching a record high of £4.5bn in the UK over the month.

Web sales increased 75 per cent year-on-year

Web sales increased 75 per cent year-on-year, amounting to the equivalent of £75 for every person in the UK, according to the IMRG Capgemini e-Retail Sales Index.

Electricals are the favourite pur-

By Julian Goldsmith

chase, followed by clothing, with 38 per cent and 32 per cent share of revenues respectively.

Anthoula Madden, head of Capgemini's UK consumer products and retail team, said online growth is happening despite sluggish sales on the high street with retailing revenues increasing by only three per cent.

Madden said: 'The results show the maturity of the online market, with consumers being more confident about buying goods online. On

Christmas day, more people were online than went to church. At the same time, the economic situation has been tough and people may have held their spending back until the January sales started this year. The growth in revenues was probably driven by seasonal discounting.'
25 February 2008

⇨ The above information is reprinted with kind permission from Silicon.com. Visit www.silicon.com for more information.

Internet shopping

Key findings

In just a few years, the Internet has had a profound impact on UK retailing, enabling businesses to sell and shoppers to buy products from anywhere in the world at any time. Internet shopping is bringing huge benefits to millions of consumers and thousands of businesses.

Our fact-finding study, however, also identified some areas where more could be done to ensure people get the most from buying online, and can feel confident and protected when doing so.

Our findings include:

⇨ Awareness of online shoppers' rights is low for businesses and consumers. Many businesses are not fully complying with laws to protect shoppers. In part, this reflects a need for higher profile guidance. There are many advisory services, but no single overall dedicated source – especially to help businesses to be aware of all they need to know when selling online.

⇨ The anonymity, speed of change and borderless nature of the Internet can pose particular challenges for the enforcers of shoppers' rights. However, new developments in the powers, roles and relationships between enforcers provide an opportunity to bring more coordination to how they can overcome these problems. In some areas, the laws that protect online shoppers also need some modernising.

⇨ Shoppers have significant fears about security and privacy, which put some off buying online altogether. Internet users who are too worried to buy online could be missing savings of £175m to £350m each year. There are risks from using the Internet generally, but it is not apparent that such high levels of fear about shopping online are warranted, provided shoppers and businesses take sensible precautions. However, awareness of these precautions, as well as the remedies available if something goes wrong, remains weak. Advice to shoppers needs to inform without scaring them.

⇨ By searching more effectively, shoppers can find big savings. We estimate these could amount to £150m to £240m each year. But they may also be hindered by unexpected additional charges which are sometimes added in the latter stages of a purchase. These charges annoy shoppers, and lead to some paying more than they might. We estimate that shoppers pay £60m to £100m a year in unexpected additional charges.

June 2007

⇨ Information from the Office of Fair Trading. Visit www.oft.gov.uk for more information.

People 'losing control' of personal information

Demos launches new report – *FYI: The New Politics of Personal Information*

People are losing control of their own personal information, according to a report launched by Demos today. People need to be put back in the driving seat when it comes to their own data and they need to be able count on a greater level of trust and openness with government and companies that hold their information.

The study, supported by O2, is the outcome of a nine-month research project into the new politics of personal information including focus groups, and individual interviews with leading figures from credit agencies, technologists, government

agencies, academics and the private sector. The launch event will take place on 7 December at 9:00am, with the Information Commissioner Richard Thomas.

Demos researcher and author of the study Peter Bradwell commented:

'We found that the people rushing to share their information through Facebook, club cards and Oyster cards when in London, were the very same people who were worried about data protection and disconnected from the way the private sector and the state make use of their information.

'People want convenience and personalised public services, but now the power is all in the hands of companies and government. People's private life becomes impersonal information once it leaves their hands.

'It's time for a political information revolution that gives the power and accountability back to the people.'

Report recommendations

⇨ The government must urgently develop a more coherent strategy around the way personal information is held and used. It must implement 'cash-handling' disciplines to ensure that personal information is treated with sufficient value and respect.

'It's time for a political information revolution that gives the power and accountability back to the people'

⇨ Government departments should have a responsibility to tell individuals how their information is used and how that affects them.

⇨ The Information Commissioner's Office needs strong new powers to 'swoop' on any organisation holding personal information and audit its use and security.

⇨ Major public projects should be road-tested for their effect on personal data with privacy impact assessments.

⇨ Belated public engagement with ID card scheme must be urgently sought now, or the scheme abandoned.

⇨ Individuals should have the right to know and contest what information about them, their finances and their lifestyle is being traded in the private sector.

⇨ Banks should consider a no-claims bonus for people who successfully protect their identity.

Peter Erskine, Chairman and CEO of Telefónica O2 Europe, said:

'I believe that business and technology has a crucial role to play in helping to address some of the challenges facing our society. Our customers are increasingly amazed by what they can do with their mobile phones, but will only take up new applications if they are sure they are safe and secure.

'We need to address these concerns as new services emerge by making sure that we protect personal information while technology drives greater data sharing. Protecting people's privacy and personal data, and preventing e-crime remains a high priority for Telefónica O2 Europe.'

7 December 2007

⇨ The above information is reprinted with kind permission from Demos. Visit www.demos.co.uk for more information.

© *Demos*

Ofcom research highlights identity fraud worry

Information from Ofcom

Concerns about identity fraud and other people using personal details have risen by 15% in two years, Ofcom research revealed today. Additionally, over two-thirds (69%) of people are concerned about the amount of personal information that companies hold about them.

However, the research also shows that more people who use the Internet are now happy to provide personal information online, for example, their credit or debit card details, than in 2005. In these cases, the research suggests that people may be making more informed decisions about a website before entering their personal details.

Although 91% of people are very or fairly confident about finding the information they want online, just 59% are confident about telling whether a website is truthful or reliable or not. The research shows that, while the majority of people do make some kind of judgement about a website before entering personal details, 11% of people do not. 16- to 24-year-olds are the most relaxed.

Although 91% of people are very or fairly confident about finding the information they want online, just 59% are confident about telling whether a website is truthful or reliable or not

---

Protecting children – television and online

There has been a significant increase in using PIN/password protection on multi-channel television in households of 8-11s since 2005 (25% to 31%) and as a result this younger age group is now more likely than 12-15s to have such restrictions to their television viewing.

There has, however, been a decline in households with Internet access having blocking software or controls regarding online access, particularly in households with older children (55% to 51% of 8-11s and 50% to 43% of 12-15s). This is mainly due to parents' beliefs in their child's ability to self-regulate their Internet behaviour. Four in five parents who have not set controls have not done so because they trust their child to be responsible.

Mobile phones

One in three adults has a concern about mobile phones. Concerns include risks to society, e.g. 'happy slapping', affordability and risks to health.

Identity fraud

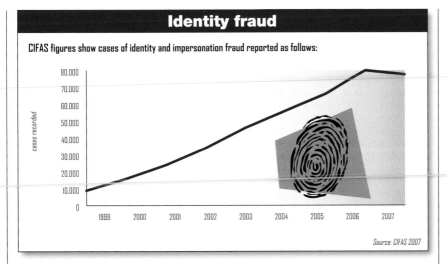

CIFAS figures show cases of identity and impersonation fraud reported as follows:

cases recorded — vertical axis labelled from 0 to 80,000 (in increments of 10,000); horizontal axis years 1999, 2000, 2001, 2002, 2003, 2004, 2005, 2006, 2007

Source: CIFAS 2007

Gaming and downloading

Although academic research to date has largely failed to demonstrate a proven link between violent games and behaviour, children appear to share the wider public concern around this issue.

Around two-thirds of older children agree that violence in games affects people's behaviour outside the game. There are high levels of agreement with controls setting age ratings for some games.

Around the same number of adults also show concern about gaming, with 68% believing that violent games can affect behaviour in the real world.

For children, awareness of online shops and free file-sharing services is high, even among non-Internet users. However, most (77%) are not aware that downloading music or videos from some file-sharing services is illegal. Of those who are aware, 50% believe that such downloads should be free.

Ofcom's Media Literacy Audits are part of a wide programme of Ofcom research into Media Literacy in the UK.

In line with Ofcom's duty to promote Media Literacy, they provide us with a base of evidence to develop new policies and initiatives to help citizens and consumers access and use digital media services and technologies.

Stewart Purvis, Ofcom's Partner for Content and Standards, said: 'This research helps Ofcom understand how people's use of digital technology has changed as it becomes ever more a part of our lives. Although we have come a long way in the past few years, we need to ensure that people are not left behind by the pace of change. In particular, Ofcom will work with its partners and stakeholders to help all citizens develop the skills, knowledge and understanding to make full use of the opportunities available and to protect themselves and their families from possible risks.'
16 May 2008

⇨ The above information is re-printed with kind permission from Ofcom. Visit www.ofcom.org.uk for more information.

© Ofcom

Phishing explained

Information from Bank Safe Online

What is phishing?

Phishing is the name given to the practice of sending emails at random purporting to come from a genuine company operating on the Internet, in an attempt to trick customers of that company into disclosing information at a bogus website operated by fraudsters. These emails usually claim that it is necessary to 'update' or 'verify' your customer account information and they urge people to click on a link from the email which takes them to the bogus website. Any information entered on the bogus website will be captured by the criminals for their own fraudulent purposes.

How can I prevent myself being a victim of phishing?

The key thing is to be suspicious of all unsolicited or unexpected emails you receive, even if they appear to originate from a trusted source. Although your bank may contact you by email, they will never ask you to reconfirm your login or security password information by clicking on a link in an email and visiting a web site. Stop to think about how your bank normally communicates with you and never disclose your password in full or personal information.

Banks will never contact you by

Phishing is the practice of sending emails at random purporting to come from a genuine company operating on the Internet, in an attempt to trick customers into disclosing information at a bogus website

email to ask you to enter your password or any other sensitive information by clicking on a link and visiting a web site. The emails are sent out completely at random in the hope of reaching a live email address of a customer with an account at the bank being targeted.

How to spot a phishing email

1 Who is the email from?
Phishing emails can look like they come from a real bank email address. Unfortunately the way Internet email works makes it a relatively simple matter for phishers to create a fake entry in the 'From:' box.

The email address that appears in the 'From' field of an email is NOT a guarantee that it came from the person or organisation that it says it did. These emails were not sent using the bank's own systems.

2 Who is the email for?
The emails are sent out at random to bulk email lists and the fraudsters will almost certainly not know your real name or indeed anything else about you, and will address you in vague terms like 'Dear Valued Customer'.

3 Take a closer look at the email – does it look 'phishy'?

The first thing to remember is that banks will never write to you and ask you for your password or any other sensitive information by email. The message is also likely to contain odd 'spe11ings' or cApitALs in the 'Subject:' box (this is an attempt to get around spam filter software), as well as grammatical and spelling errors.

Never log on to your online banking account by clicking on a link in an email. Open your web browser and type the bank's address in yourself.

If in any doubt about the validity of an email purporting to come from your bank, contact them on an advertised phone number.

⇨ The above information is re-printed with kind permission from Bank Safe Online. Visit www.banksafeonline.org.uk for more information.

© BankSafeOnline

Spyware and adware

Information from CyberAngels

What is spyware/adware?
Spyware is a type of program that gathers personal information from your computer and relays it back to another computer, generally for advertising purposes. These programs can also change your computer's configuration, force open ads or redirect your browser.

Often, when you download free-ware and shareware programs (such as Kazaa or Wild Tangent), you unknowingly trigger adware by accepting an End User License Agreement.

Why is spyware dangerous?
Adware and spyware not only pose privacy and security threats, these programs substantially slow down your computer because of the enormous amount of resources required to process and transmit data (and open all of those pop-up windows!). Oftentimes, your computer is not able to process legitimate programs because of the toll these programs are

taking on your computer. Aside from your computer crashing, these types of programs may leave security holes that make your computer susceptible to exploitation by hackers.

How do you know if there is spyware on your computer?
Your computer may exhibit some or many of these symptoms:
⇨ Endless pop-up windows.
⇨ Your home page has changed.
⇨ Strange toolbars on your browser.
⇨ Unfamiliar icons in your taskbar.
⇨ Your computer is sluggish, and has a hard time opening programs or saving files.

How can you prevent spyware from being installed on your computer?
⇨ Be wary of free downloads.
⇨ Always read the End User License Agreement before installing new programs.
⇨ Don't click on links within pop-up windows (click the 'X' icon in the

titlebar to close).
⇨ Adjust your browser preferences to limit cookies and pop-up windows.
⇨ Install an Anti-Spyware Program.

⇨ The above information is re-printed with kind permission from CyberAngels. Visit www.cyberangels.org for more information.

© CyberAngels

Some spyware can permanently damage a computer

Cybercrime committed every 10 seconds

Blackmail, threats and online fraud

Cybercrime is on the rise with a UK victim hit every 10 seconds, figures suggested today.

A report claims that more than 3 million online offences were committed last year as perpetrators increasingly hide behind the anonymity of the Internet.

In nearly two-thirds of cases the intended target was an individual as opposed to a firm, with abusive emails and online identity theft among the crimes being identified.

A study commissioned by online identity firm Garlik found that 60% of the estimated 3,237,500 cybercrimes committed in 2006 were 'offences against the person'.

Blackmail

These included threatening emails, blackmail perpetrated over the Internet and online fraud.

More than 200,000 cases of financial fraud were recorded in 2006, with criminals impersonating the victim to obtain money, credit or a better job, the report said.

Cases of online harassment during 2006 numbered almost two million, the report claims.

The study, compiled by online criminology firm 1871 Ltd, reports that the relative anonymity and 'safe' distance that the Internet allows is driving a wave of cybercrime.

But many offences are going unreported. It is claimed that 90% of online harassment is carried out without a formal complaint being made.

Unwanted sexual approaches over the Internet accounted for 850,000 of last year's cybercrime, according to the report.

Online chatrooms

In the same period 238 offences of meeting a child following sexual grooming through an online chatroom were recorded.

The report is based on data from official sources and quantitative and qualitative research using a sample of 200 cyber criminals.

Stefan Fafinski, author of the report, said: 'Although measuring cybercrime is difficult, it is clear that in many instances it is outstripping "traditional" crime.

'This is a result of unparalleled opportunities that the Internet gives both for making familiar crimes easier and enabling "pure" cybercrimes that could not exist without the Internet.'

He added: 'If it remains unchecked it will continue to increase.'

6 September 2007

Downloading

Downloading from the Internet can be a minefield. To avoid viruses, bankruptcy and, potentially, a spell in prison, read TheSite's guide to downloading media

What's downloading?

Downloading is the process of transferring data – be it music, video, software or information – from a computer or server elsewhere on the Internet to yours.

By far the most controversial downloaded material is music, although as video downloading rises it is becoming just as hot a topic. The controversy arises from the source of the downloads and the copyright issues involved.

Why, what's the problem?

A lot of online music and video is copyrighted, so it's illegal for anyone to reproduce it in order to supply it to someone else. Just as copying

By Simon Easterman

albums on to tape or minidisk has always been illegal, so is sharing digital files containing copyrighted material over the web. By law, a financial contribution should go to the writers and distributors of the material every time it is reproduced.

So do I have to pay for all the music and films I download?

Only if it's copyrighted. There is a lot of freely distributed stuff out there, from musicians and filmmakers who just want to get their work to an audience. It won't all be great but it's worth looking at. Check out

ArtistDirect, or CreativeCommons. MySpace is also an excellent source of legal free music. There are some blogs and podcasts that make a point of only playing free music.

As for copyrighted material, if you want to stay legal, you need to pay for your music and movies. Legitimate sites such as iTunes, eMusic and Napster are all set up to help you do this.

How do these sites work and how do I choose the best one for me?

They all work slightly differently – make sure that the music they offer, the price and the method of payment suits you.

⇨ Most major sites let you browse

— nothing here —

YOUR CHOICE:

LEGAL

CRIMINAL

their catalogues, which can vary widely. Make sure a site's selling stuff you want before signing up.
⇨ Look for a site that lets you listen to excerpts of tunes before you buy them. Most do, so it's daft not to.
⇨ Sites generally offer either a subscription or a pay-per-song model. Think about how much music you're likely to be buying and which method will give you the best value. You should compare rates between sites as well.
⇨ As with all online transactions, make sure the payment page is secure (with https:// at the beginning of the address). Use a credit card if you can, preferably one you keep solely for use on the web (so if your details do fall into the wrong hands, any large losses will be covered by the credit card company).
⇨ If you have a portable digital music player, make sure the file format the site provides will be compatible with it.
⇨ All sites have their own approach to something called 'digital rights management' (DRM). Basically, this sets out what you can and can't do with the files once you download them. For example, some systems only allow you to copy the file five times; some will stop the files working at all if you stop paying a subscription.
⇨ Take an interest what 'bit-rate' the files are sold in (such as 128kbps or 256kbps). This refers to how much the original file has been 'compressed'. Highly-compressed files will download faster, but the sound quality isn't as good.

⇨ Get broadband – your downloading will be far quicker and less likely to fail due to a dodgy connection.

What's peer-to-peer downloading?

Peer-to-peer (P2P), or filesharing, software which can be obtained from sites such as Kazaa, Gnutella and Morpheus, allows you to search other users' computers and download material from them. Rather than offering the material from the website's server, it gives you access to the resources of hundreds or thousands of fellow Internet users' PCs, for free. You in turn, offer your files to others for download from your computer.

Sounds great, what's wrong with that?

Firstly, due to the copyright issues involved, most use of P2P is illegal. It might seem a small-time offence to you but the music and film industries take it very seriously. The Recording Industry Association of America (RIAA) and the British Phonographic Industry (BPI) (not to mention the Motion Picture Association of America (MPAA)) are doing their best to bring enthusiastic filesharers to justice and there have been several convictions on both sides of the Atlantic. The RIAA, in particular, has been filing lawsuits against schools, universities and families it says have broken copyright law.

Also, when you download P2P software, it can bring with it other unwanted programs. Some P2P software brings spyware or viruses with them, which can steal your information or damage your computer.

And bear in mind that the software allows other people to search your computer as well. Financial details and personal documents could be downloaded off your computer if you leave the door open.

If you are going to do P2P downloading, the safest option is to use a dedicated PC with as little else on its hard drive as possible and a full compliment of firewalls, anti-spyware and antivirus programs, all kept up to date.

What about BitTorrent?

BitTorrent is P2P Mark II. It is filesharing software that enables far faster downloading speeds, so you can get larger files in a fraction of the time. When you search for a file in BitTorrent, instead of identifying one potential filesharer, the software finds lots of different users' computers that have the file on their hard drive. It then takes a different bit of the file from each of these users and downloads it to your machine. The software then reassembles all the bits, and you have the entire file.

The advantage of this is that it takes far less time to transport lots of little files over multiple lines than one big file over one line. In fact the software can actually detect Internet traffic, and find quieter lines to download across, thus avoiding bottlenecks and getting the best download speed. The real impact of BitTorrent is to make obtaining large files (like films) through the P2P networks a far more workable option.

BitTorrent is, by most accounts, a lot 'safer' than earlier P2P systems. However, it is still illegal if the file contains copyrighted material.

Don't let that put you off finding and downloading the legal, free stuff. The web is bursting with great music and video that you can download legally and without paying a penny. You just have to search a bit harder for it. Have a look at rcrdlbl, Elbows, and Hype Machine.

⇨ The above information is re-printed with kind permission from TheSite. Visit www.thesite.org for more information.

© TheSite

Wi-Fi hijacking common crime

Information from PC Pro

By Stuart Turton

Over half of computer users have admitted to piggy-backing a wireless Internet connection without permission, says a new survey.

According to Sophos, Wi-Fi hijacking is generally a crime of opportunity with the majority of those surveyed having logged on to a local network simply because it wasn't properly secured with encryption keys.

'My suspicion would be that most people don't know what they're doing,' says Graham Cluley, senior technology consultant for Sophos.

'They're in a hotel lobby trying to log on and one option asks for their room number and password and then they see another one, which doesn't and they think, hang-on. I don't think it's necessarily done maliciously, it's just easy.

'But their neighbours can lose out if their bandwidth is gobbled up by freeloaders downloading pirated copies of *Heroes* Season Two from the net all day long.'

Wi-Fi freeloading is a crime the police take extremely seriously due to the anonymity it affords criminals, and perpetrators currently face a maximum fine of £1,000 and a five-year sentence.

However, the crime is difficult to track and only a handful of arrests have been made.

Despite that, a recent survey by GetSafeOnline reveals that there are around 7.8 million unsecured wireless connections in the UK.

16 November 2007

⇨ The above information is re-printed with kind permission from PC Pro. Visit www.pcpro.co.uk for more information.

© PC Pro

Censoring of Internet is 'spreading like virus'

By Richard Spencer in Beijing

Dozens of countries are copying China's methods of censoring the Internet, Amnesty International said yesterday.

In advance of a live webcast to discuss Internet freedom, Amnesty gave warning that censorship was a 'virus' that was infecting countries round the world.

Tim Hancock, Amnesty's international campaigns director, said: 'The "Chinese model" of an Internet that allows economic growth but not free speech or privacy is growing in popularity, from a handful of countries five years ago to dozens of governments today who block sites and arrest bloggers.'

China's 144 million Internet users face the most sophisticated controls in the world. Software filters hundreds of millions of emails, web-pages, and mobile phone text messages for key words that trigger either automatic blocks or further investigation by censors.

In addition, Internet companies in China, including overseas firms, have to operate systems of self-censorship. The Chinese government claims that the rules are in line with international norms for countering crime such as pornography, but does not deny that they also cover political activity.

> **'The "Chinese model" of an Internet that allows economic growth but not free speech or privacy is growing in popularity'**

Shi Tao, an award-winning reporter on a central Chinese newspaper, is serving 10 years in jail for sending details of one censorship order to Human Rights in China by email.

His details were handed over to police by the American Internet firm Yahoo!. Amnesty said such practices could change the Internet 'beyond all recognition' as they are taken up by other countries.

It cited research by an academic study group, the Open Net Initiative, that at least 25 governments employed filtering for censorship. They included Iran, Burma, and Saudi Arabia but also Western-oriented democracies such as India and South Korea.

The webcast discussion will feature Martha Lane-Fox, the dotcom entrepreneur, and Jimmy Wales, the founder of Wikipedia, the Internet encyclopedia, which is one of thousands of sites permanently blocked in China.

8 June 2007

© Telegraph Group Limited, London 2008

Addiction to Internet 'is an illness'

New evidence shows that heavy users suffer isolation, fatigue and withdrawal symptoms

By David Smith, Technology Correspondent

Tense? Angry? Can't get online? Internet addiction is now a serious public health issue that should be officially recognised as a clinical disorder, according to a leading psychiatrist.

Excessive gaming, viewing online pornography, emailing and text messaging have been identified as causes of a compulsive-impulsive disorder by Dr Jerald Block, author of an editorial for the respected *American Journal of Psychiatry*. Block argues that the disorder is now so common that it merits inclusion in the *Diagnostic and Statistical Manual of Mental Disorders*, the profession's primary resource to categorise and diagnose mental illnesses. He says Internet addiction has four main components:

⇨ Excessive use, often associated with a loss of sense of time or a neglect of basic drives;

⇨ Withdrawal, including feelings of anger, tension and/or depression when the computer is inaccessible;

⇨ The need for better computers, more software, or more hours of use;

⇨ Negative repercussions, including arguments, lying, poor achievement, social isolation and fatigue.

A primary case study is South Korea, which has the greatest use of broadband in the world. Block points out that 10 people died from blood clots from remaining seated for long periods in Internet cafes and another was murdered because of an online game. Their country now 'considers Internet addiction one of its most serious public health issues'. The government estimates that around 210,000 South Korean children are affected and in need of treatment, of whom 80 per cent might need drugs targeting the brain and nearly a quarter could need to go to hospital. Since the average high school pupil there spends about 23 hours per week gaming, Block notes, another 1.2 million are believed to be at risk of addiction and require basic counselling. There has been alarm over a rising number of addicts dropping out of school or quitting their jobs to spend more time on computers. In China it has been reported that 13.7 per cent of adolescent Internet users, about 10 million, could be considered addicts.

Block, a psychiatrist at the Oregon Health & Science University in Portland, writes that the extent of the disorder is more difficult to estimate in America because people tend to surf at home instead of in Internet cafes. But he believes there are similar cases, concluding: 'Unfortunately Internet addiction is resistant to treatment, entails significant risks and has high relapse rates.' He told *The Observer* that he did not believe specific websites were responsible. 'The relationship is with the computer,' he said. 'First, it becomes a significant other to them. Second, they exhaust emotions that they could experience in the real world on the computer, through any number of mechanisms: emailing, gaming, porn. Third, computer use occupies a tremendous amount of time in their life. Then if you try to cut the cord in a very abrupt fashion, they've lost essentially their best friend. That can take the form of depression or rage.'

Harry Husted, a single 51-year-old from New York, spends 16 hours a day on the Internet. He insists that he is not addicted, but admits that he used to be. 'I used to work with computers for eight hours, then get home and go online for seven hours. I would stay up till two or three in the morning until I got so sleepy I had to go to bed. I wouldn't go out to get the groceries and I couldn't have cared less about friends, TV, anything. After a while I realised what was happening and did something about it. Now if I use MySpace it's only to advertise my business.'

Internet addiction clinics have sprung up around the world in an attempt to wean people off their need for a fix. Many people have turned, apparently without irony, to web discussion boards with names such as Internet Addicts Anonymous. The Centre for Internet Addiction Recovery in Bradford, Pennsylvania, says Internet addiction has become a growing legal issue in criminal, divorce and employment cases. It offers a consultation service to lawyers that includes 'assessing the role of electronic anonymity in the development of deviant, deceptive and illegal sexual online activities'.

Robert Freedman, editor of the *American Journal of Psychiatry*, said expressions of the addiction could be diverse. 'In Korea, it seems to be primarily gaming sites. In America, it seems to be Facebook. It's porn, it's games, it's gambling, it's chatting with friends. All these things existed before, but now they're a lot easier.'

To beat the addiction, he advised: 'A self-help group might be a place to start. Maybe replace an online group with a real one.'

Are you a net junkie?

If you answer 'yes' to five or more of these questions, you may have an Internet addiction.

⇨ Do you feel preoccupied with the Internet? (Think about your online activity or anticipate your next online session.)

⇨ Do you need increasing amounts of time on the net in order to achieve satisfaction?

⇨ Have you repeatedly made unsuccessful efforts to control, cut back or stop Internet use?

⇨ Do you feel restless, moody, depressed, or irritable when attempting to cut down or stop Internet use?

⇨ Do you stay online longer than originally intended?

⇨ Have you jeopardised or risked the loss of a significant relationship, job, educational or career opportunity because of the Internet?

⇨ Have you lied to family members, a therapist or others to conceal the extent of your involvement with the Internet?

⇨ Do you use it to escape from problems (e.g. feelings of helplessness, guilt, anxiety, depression)?

Source: Centre for Internet Addiction Recovery netaddiction.com

⇨ This article first appeared in *The Observer*, 23 March 2008

© *Guardian Newspapers Limited 2008*

Online gaming addiction

Information from the US Center for Internet Addiction

Online gaming addiction is an addiction to online video games, role-playing games, or any interactive gaming environment available through the Internet. Online games such 'EverQuest', the 'World of Warcraft', the 'Dark Age of Camelot', or 'Diablo II' – dubbed 'heroinware' by some players – can pose much more complex problems. Extensive chat features give such games a social aspect missing from offline activities, and the collaborative/competitive nature of working with or against other players can make it hard to take a break.

A new parental concern

Parents across the globe are increasingly concerned about their sons' and daughters' online gaming habits. They are sure that there is a problem but counsellors unfamiliar with online gaming addiction don't understand how seductive they can be. One mother explained that she had talked to her son's guidance counsellors, the school psychologist, and two local addiction rehabilitation centres. 'No one had ever heard of someone getting addicted to Xbox Live,' she said. 'They all told me it was a phase and that I should try to limit my son's game playing. They didn't understand that I couldn't. He had lost touch with reality. My son lost interest in everything else. He didn't want to eat, sleep, or go to school, the game was the only thing that mattered to him.'

Parents often feel alone and scared as their children become hooked to something that no one seems to understand. 'My son's counsellor told me to just turn off the computer,' another mother explained. 'That was like telling the parent of an alcoholic son to tell him to just stop drinking. It wasn't that simple. We felt like no one was taking us seriously that our son had a real problem.'

Signs of addiction

Gamers who become hooked show clear signs of addiction. Like a drug, gamers who play almost every day, play for extended periods of time (over 4 hours), get restless or irritable if they can't play, and sacrifice other social activities just to game are showing signs of addiction.

Warning signs include:

⇨ A preoccupation with gaming.

⇨ Lying or hiding gaming use.

⇨ Disobedience at time limits.

⇨ Social withdrawal from family and friends.

⇨ Information from the Center for Internet Addiction. Visit www. netaddiction.com for more.

© *Center for Internet Addiction*

Chinese gamer dies after three-day session

Information from vnunet.com

A 30-year-old man has died in the south China province of Guangzhou after apparently playing an online game continuously for three days.

Reports in *Beijing News* said that the man suddenly collapsed and was rushed to hospital. Doctors were unable to revive him.

'Police have ruled out the possibility of suicide,' the newspaper said, adding that 'exhaustion' was the most likely cause of death.

The name of the Internet cafe has not been released, nor the game that the Guangzhou resident was playing.

The 30-year-old is not the first to die after prolonged Internet use. Earlier this year Xu Yan, a local teacher from Jinzhou in Liaoning province, collapsed after spending almost 15 days playing online games.

The Chinese government is taking an increasingly tough line on 'Internet addiction', including boot camps to get people to use the Internet less and the use of electrotherapy.

By Iain Thomson
17 September 2007

⇨ The above information is reprinted with kind permission from vnunet. com. Visit www.vnunet.com for more information.

© *vnunet.com*

⇨ More than 304 million people now have broadband access worldwide, out of a total of 1.24 billion Internet users, though it's worth remembering that this also shows that any kind of access is still a relative privilege: as of 2007, 81% of the world's population has no home connection. (page 1)

⇨ April 30 2008 is the 15th birthday of the world wide web; specifically, this date marks the 15th anniversary of CERN (the European Organisation for Nuclear Research) announcing that the web was free for use by anyone. (page 2)

⇨ The most popular online activity in Europe, according to an EIAA survey, was searching, followed by email and communicating via social networking sites. (page 3)

⇨ Over 75% of 11-year-olds now have their own television, games console and mobile phone. Some 15% of 13- to 15-year-olds and 7% of 10-year-olds also have their own webcam. (page 4)

⇨ Adults who live with children are more engaged online than those who don't, indicating that family needs and wants are shaping web behaviour. (page 7)

⇨ Nearly half of all children who have access to the Internet have their own personal profile on a social networking site, according to Ofcom research. (page 9)

⇨ As many as four and a half million young people (71%) would not want a college, university or potential employer to conduct an Internet search on them unless they could first remove content from social networking sites, according to research by the Information Commissioner's Office (ICO). But almost six in ten have never considered that what they put online now might be permanent and could be accessed years into the future. (page 10)

⇨ Almost half (44%) of UK mobile phone subscribers belong to an online social network. Of this group, one in four (25%) use their mobile phone for social networking-related activities. (page 11)

⇨ 94% of British youngsters own mobile phones compared to 80% in the US. (page 12)

⇨ British youth are really prolific texters with 50% sending more than six every day. (page 13)

⇨ The 30.6 million Britons active online in June 2007 spent a total of 31.8 billion minutes surfing the web and using Internet-related applications – an average of 17 hours 21 minutes per active Briton online. (page 15)

⇨ 'Geek speak' has become the fastest-growing language in Europe as new words are invented to describe technological advances. (page 16)

⇨ More than nine out of ten connections to the Internet are via broadband. (page 17)

⇨ The government is to spend £30m over the next three years to bring broadband access to schoolchildren and low-income families. (page 18)

⇨ Internet plagiarism is a major problem among sixth-form pupils according to over half the teachers questioned in an Association of Teachers and Lecturers (ATL) survey. (page 19)

⇨ Almost 21 million Britons visited a TV, video or movie-related website in Sept 2007 – a 28% increase in visitors since Sept 2006. (page 21)

⇨ Many young people are effectively being 'raised online' spending in excess of 20 hours a week using sites such as Bebo, MySpace, Facebook and YouTube, according to research. (page 27)

⇨ Children's illicit online activity is putting them in danger, with parents totally oblivious to this high-risk behaviour, according to new research. (page 28)

⇨ Electricals are the favourite online purchase, followed by clothing, with 38 per cent and 32 per cent share of revenues respectively. (page 30)

⇨ Concerns about identity fraud and other people using personal details have risen by 15% in two years, Ofcom research has revealed. Additionally, over two-thirds (69%) of people are concerned about the amount of personal information that companies hold about them. (page 32)

⇨ Cybercrime is on the rise with a UK victim hit every 10 seconds. (page 35)

⇨ Over half of computer users have admitted to piggy-backing a wireless Internet connection without permission, says a new survey. (page 37)

⇨ Dozens of countries are copying China's methods of censoring the Internet, Amnesty International has said. (page 37)

⇨ Internet addiction is now a serious public health issue that should be officially recognised as a clinical disorder, according to a leading psychiatrist. (page 38)

GLOSSARY

'Blog'
An abbreviation of 'web log'. This is an online journal or diary recording an individual's opinions, activities and/or events in their lives.

Broadband
High-speed Internet connection which allows a large amount of data to be transmitted. This is now the most popular way of connecting to the Internet in the UK, having overtaken dial-up (a much slower method of accessing the Internet via a telephone line) in 2005.

Censorship
Preventing the expression of certain information and opinions. In terms of the Internet, this is a controversial issue: some feel greater censorship of the Internet in the UK would be a valuable step towards protecting children online; however, others fear this would lead to the loss of online freedom of speech. In some countries, such as China, the government uses censorship to prevent the country's Internet users from accessing websites which are critical of its policies.

Cybercrime
A crime committed using a computer or the Internet. Common cybercrimes include identity theft, hacking and downloading data illegally. It is estimated that in the UK someone is a victim of cybercrime every 10 seconds.

Cyberspace
A term coined to describe the virtual world created by the Internet.

Dotcom
A business operating mainly via the Internet. The URLs of business websites often end in .com. This term was popular during the so-called 'dotcom boom' of the 1990s, but is used less frequently now.

Download
To transfer data from an Internet-connected computer or server on to your own. Copyright laws mean that it is illegal to download certain copyrighted media, for example music and films, without the consent of the creator. Most legal downloads require payment, although some non-copyrighted content is available for free. Illegal downloading is one of the most common online crimes.

Internet
An enormous global computer network over which the world wide web is accessed.

Internet addiction
A compulsive-impulsive disorder associated with excessive use of the Internet or online games. Sufferers experience withdrawal symptoms when they cannot go online. Certain online games, dubbed 'heroinware', have been particularly associated with addictive behaviour.

'Nerdic'
Refers to the ever-growing language used to describe technological advances. Experts claim about 100 new words are added to 'Nerdic' every year.

Phishing
Fraudulent attempts to obtain information by sending emails purporting to come from a genuine company, such as a bank. They often ask the receiver to 'update' or 'verify' account information which they then use for fraudulent purposes. It is important to remember never to reply to an email claiming to come from your bank or to visit any links within it: contact the bank directly if you want to know more about the email.

Search engine
A program that searches for information available on the web. Users can enter their search criteria and the search engine will return a list of pages that match the query.

Social networking
A way to interact and communicate with other people through sites such as MySpace or Facebook. Each user has a profile containing personal information, photos and other data which their online friends can view.

Spyware/adware
A program that is installed on a user's computer without their knowledge and collects information on the user, usually for advertising purposes.

The world wide web
The world wide web (often called just 'the web') refers to the interlinked documents which can be viewed over the Internet.

Web 2.0
A term used to describe what is perceived as the second generation of the Internet, which involved a shift towards user-generated content. Web 2.0 is characterised by tools which allow users to interact and collaborate online, such as social networking sites and blogs, where the content is actually shaped by the users.

Wi-Fi
Wireless network connection.

Wiki
A website that allows users to create and edit content.

INDEX

Additional Resources

Other Issues titles

If you are interested in researching further some of the issues raised in *The Internet Revolution*, you may like to read the following titles in the **Issues** series:

⇨ Vol. 157 *The Problem of Globalisation* (ISBN 978 1 86168 444 8)

⇨ Vol. 156 *Travel and Tourism* (ISBN 978 1 86168 443 1)

⇨ Vol. 142 *Media Issues* (ISBN 978 1 86168 408 0)

⇨ Vol. 132 *Child Abuse* (ISBN 978 1 86168 378 6)

⇨ Vol. 129 *Gambling Trends* (ISBN 978 1 86168 375 5)

⇨ Vol. 122 *Bullying* (ISBN 978 1 86168 361 8)

⇨ Vol. 121 *The Censorship Debate* (ISBN 978 1 86168 354 0)

⇨ Vol. 82 *Protecting our Privacy* (ISBN 978 1 86168 277 2)

For more information about these titles, visit our website at www.independence.co.uk/publicationslist

Useful organisations

You may find the websites of the following organisations' websites useful for further research:

⇨ **Bank Safe Online:** www.banksafeonline.org.uk

⇨ **Center for Internet Addiction:** www.netaddiction.com

⇨ **Computing:** www.computing.co.uk

⇨ **CyberAngels:** www.cyberangels.org

⇨ **EIAA:** www.eiaa.net

⇨ **Garlik:** www.garlik.com

⇨ **Nielsen Online:** www.nielsen-netratings.com

⇨ **Ofcom:** www.ofcom.org.uk

⇨ **PC Pro:** www.pcpro.co.uk

⇨ **Sharpened Glossary:** www.sharpened.net/glossary

⇨ **vnunet:** www.vnunet.com

⇨ **ZDNet:** www.zdnet.co.uk

ACKNOWLEDGEMENTS

The publisher is grateful for permission to reproduce the following material.

While every care has been taken to trace and acknowledge copyright, the publisher tenders its apology for any accidental infringement or where copyright has proved untraceable. The publisher would be pleased to come to a suitable arrangement in any such case with the rightful owner.

Chapter One: The Changing Web

The Internet, © Guardian Newspapers Ltd, *15 years of the world wide web*, © MSN, *The communications revolution*, © Ofcom, *Web 2.0*, © Sharpened Glossary, *Internet's a family affair*, © European Interactive Advertising Association, *Blogging*, © TheSite, *Ofcom research identifies social networking profiles*, © Crown copyright is reproduced with the permission of Her Majesty's Stationery Office, *Social networking and your electronic footprint*, © Crown copyright is reproduced with the permission of Her Majesty's Stationery Office, *Social networking is going mobile*, © Nielsen Online, *Mobile Life Report 2008: the connected world*, © Carphone Warehouse, *What do Britons spend the most time doing online?*, © Nielsen Online, *'Nerdic' is fastest-growing language*, © Telegraph Group Ltd, *Internet connectivity*, © Crown copyright is reproduced with the permission of Her Majesty's Stationery Office, *Government aims to bridge digital divide*, © Incisive Media Ltd, *School work plagued by net plagiarism*, © Association of Teachers and Lecturers, *Time to trust the digital generation says think tank*, © Demos, *Online TV, video and movie consumption almost doubles*, © Nielsen Online, *Microsoft to get touchy with next OS*, © Reuters, *Gates convinced speech will replace keyboards*, © PC Pro, *Internet 'to hit full capacity by 2010'*, © CNET Networks Inc., *Tim Berners-Lee: the web that thinks*, © Telegraph Group Ltd.

Chapter Two: Risks and Dangers

A generation of youth are being raised online, © Institute for Public Policy Research, *UK kids take online risks behind closed doors*, © Garlik, *Safer children in a digital world*, © Crown copyright is reproduced with the permission of Her Majesty's Stationery Office, *Online shopping reaches record high*, © CNET Networks Inc., *Internet shopping*, © Crown copyright is reproduced with the permission of Her Majesty's Stationery Office, *People 'losing control' of personal information*, © Demos, *Ofcom research highlights identity fraud worry*, © Ofcom, *Phishing explained*, © BankSafeOnline, *Spyware and adware*, © CyberAngels, *Cybercrime committed every 10 seconds*, © The Press Association, *Downloading*, © TheSite, *Wi-Fi hijacking common crime*, © PC Pro, *Censoring of Internet is 'spreading like virus'*, © Telegraph Group Ltd, *Addiction to Internet 'is an illness'*, © Guardian Newspapers Ltd, *Online gaming addiction*, © Center for Internet Addiction, *Chinese gamer dies after three-day session*, © vnunet.com.

Photographs

Stock Xchng: pages 5 (Steve Woods); 13 (Päivi Rytivaara); 23 (Vivek Chugh); 34a (Dan Mulligan); 34b (Sanja Gjenero).
Wikimedia Commons: page 34b (Husky).

Illustrations

Pages 2, 20, 29: Simon Kneebone; pages 4, 16: Bev Aisbett; pages 14, 26, 33: Don Hatcher; pages 15, 28, 36: Angelo Madrid.

Additional editorial by Claire Owen, on behalf of Independence Educational Publishers.

And with thanks to the team: Mary Chapman, Sandra Dennis, Claire Owen and Jan Sunderland.

Lisa Firth
Cambridge
September, 2008